PROJECT INSPIRED

PROJECT♥ INSPIRED

Tips and Tricks for Staying True to Who You Are

Nicole Weider

with Kristin Billerbeck

ZONDERVAN®

ZONDERVAN

Project Inspired
Copyright © 2015 by Nicole Wieder

Requests for information should be addressed to:

Zondervan, 3900 *Sparks Drive SE, Grand Rapids, Michigan 49546*

ISBN 978-0-310-74939-4

Cover design: Mind Over Media, LLC
Interior design: Kris Nelson
Photos: William Dick, Shutterstock, iStock
Fashion Stylist: Amy Ramirez
Makeup Artist: Jessica Hoffman
Photo on p. 108: ©Troy Daily News, Anthony Weber/AP Photo

Printed in China

15 16 17 18 19 20 21 22 23 24 25 26/DSC/16 15 14 13 12 11 10 9 8 7 6 5 4 3 2 1

TABLE OF CONTENTS

FOREWORD

If you had asked me seven years ago what I pictured myself doing in the future, I certainly wouldn't have said creating a ministry for teenage Christian girls. Back then, I didn't know the nature of God. I had a vague idea that He was real, but I didn't follow Jesus or have any kind of relationship with Him. The only time I had ever really gone to church was with my grandmother when I was four years old. I knew the Sunday school songs we sang, but the Bible and God's Word never crossed my mind as I got older. I relied on my own will and plans to pursue modeling and acting, because back then I thought money and fame would bring me happiness and meaning. But I know God was working in my life even when I wasn't following Him. I am so thankful now that I endured and overcame some incredibly tumultuous events while chasing my dreams in Hollywood, because unbeknownst to me, He was carrying me through each trial, knowing every struggle would ultimately bring Him glory and praise once I did become a Christian. It's through that pain and God's gift of redemption that I could in turn create this book and hopefully inspire you along the way.

My first prayer, at four years old.

Tough circumstances and hard decisions will inevitably come your way, and my hope is that this book will bless you, and that you will learn from my experiences when it comes to dealing with boys, friends, the media, fashion, and everyday life. What

I hope you take away most, however, is what I share in my testimony—that our lives can miraculously change for the better when we give up control and let God take over. He sees our eternal future, including what's best for us, and helps us get where we are meant to be. I promise you that when you make the decision to follow Him and let Him guide you, your journey in life will become more meaningful and your happiness will not be short-lived.

I often get asked about my love for makeup, beauty, and fashion, and receive questions on whether these interests are biblical, and if it is okay to care so much about our appearances. I want to share with you that it's more than okay to enjoy and wear things that make us feel beautiful. I believe that God gave us natural talents and passions for a reason. As Christians, we must live in the world, and not be sheltered from it. And whether we like it or not, how we present ourselves to the world portrays a message. For instance, it's often the case that how we dress in a job interview matters, and how we carry ourselves can help us catch the attention of someone who is a worthy husband so that he can get to know our personality. And while your main focus should always be on your relationship with God, you can also have fun dressing nicely and taking care of yourself in order to feel more confident. With that in mind, I've included my favorite items, from skin care to fashion ideas, to help you look and feel your best.

So relax, get comfortable, and enjoy this book, because it's for you!

God bless,

Nicole

What Does It Mean to Live a Project Inspired Life?

♥

THE PROJECT INSPIRED GIRL

1. Loves God with her whole heart, mind, and soul.

2. Is kind and compassionate to others.

3. Doesn't settle for a guy who doesn't treat her like God's daughter.

4. Seeks to please God instead of the world.

5. Has beauty that comes from within.

6. Cares for her body as a temple, as a gift from God.

7. Is honest about who she is and seeks truth.

8. Is generous and giving.

9. Discerns good from evil.

10. Is patient, listens, and loves relentlessly.

11. Quickly forgives and prays for her enemies.

CHAPTER 1
WHERE IS YOUR STAR?

WHERE IS YOUR STAR?

Hollywood has a series of stars on its sidewalks
branded with the names of those who have attained
worldly fame. It may sound glamorous, and there's
nothing wrong with wanting to receive one of those
plaques, but I'm here to tell you the truth: I've met
many of the celebrities on the Walk of Fame, and
although they have achieved everything that the media places importance on—such as
power, success, money, and fame—all of their achievements and awards still don't give
them the lasting fulfillment and love that they seek. On the contrary; since I became
a Christian and gave my life to Christ, I've seen joy and unspeakable radiance from
others around me who love God like I do. At the same time, I have also met people in the
entertainment industry who *are* making a great impact for the world and who still follow
Jesus. So is it possible to have both worldly success and a solid, life-affirming faith?

I think it can be, as long as you value the spiritual achievements over the worldly ones.
Because rather than receiving a star on an unclean Hollywood sidewalk, God wants our
names printed in His Book of Life. How awesome is that? It's the kind of goal we should set
for ourselves because it's eternal and cannot be washed away by wear and tear.

When I was young, my hopes and dreams were that one day I would have a star on the
Hollywood Walk of Fame. I didn't know it at the time, but that dream would lead me down
a destructive path filled with heartbreak and lost dignity. I've realized now, after the pain
I went through, that the dream I had from the beginning was actually an internal drive to
honor God in what I did, and not the world. You see, when we pursue our dream in our own
timing and not God's, roadblocks will be set up and doors will be closed. Is this rejection for
us, or just God's master plan at work in our life?

I was born in Portland, Oregon, and my dream of success started when I was six. I would watch *Sesame Street, Barney,* and *The Muppet Show.* I used to dance and sing along with the kids, which I'm sure you might have done as well. (Who can forget the "I Love You" song Barney sang at the end? I think that song is ingrained in us for life!) But I took it a step further and begged my mom to get me an agent. The market was small in Portland, but there were still some opportunities for commercials and catalog work. And when I was young, I was able to work pretty easily by doing modeling jobs and print ads. However, when puberty set in, things changed big time. I guess my bad acne and braces didn't help in the modeling department. However, my dream of performing never left me.

When I was fourteen, I booked a billboard ad for a big radio station (advertising the concept that I went on a date and it wasn't good, but as soon as I heard a good song, it made everything better). That was the beginning of my exposure to the sexualization of the modeling industry—and because I was just a teenager, and still vulnerable, I didn't understand that I was being marketed as "sexy." I was just extremely happy I was getting work.

Here's a picture of me in eighth grade, when I was on the basketball team. I got made fun of because I was really skinny and tall.

That radio billboard ad was the spark that made me want to finally move to Hollywood and pursue a fulltime modelling career in the big leagues. My family and I moved to Los Angeles when I was a junior in high school, which is a really tough time to transfer into a new school for anybody. I didn't know a single person the day I started class. In addition, the high school was double the size of my previous one, and the students were quite different from my old school—they had designer clothes, fancy cars, extravagant homes, and social circles that were impossible to break in to.

I was an outsider, and the popular girls at my school made sure I knew it. I remember one time I sat down at a bench in the middle of the quad (which was where everyone ate lunch at school), and one of the popular girls told me that I had to get up and move because the table wasn't mine.

I struggled to find my place in this new, foreign world. I tried bouncing around different groups, seeing if I was accepted. After getting to know one girl and becoming friends, she invited me to start smoking pot with her before football games. I was never into drugs, and I told her I didn't want to start. From that point on she stopped wanting to hang out with me. Then, when I was particularly down and was certain I'd made a huge mistake moving to this new school, I met my friend Christina, who was in the same drama class as me. She was so welcoming and made me feel as if I belonged. Isn't it amazing how one person can make such a huge difference in your perspective?

We were both outgoing, light-hearted, and enjoyed performing. However, the big difference between Christina and me was that she had been raised in a Christian home and I'd actually never met anyone whose faith affected their entire outlook on things. I considered myself a good person, and I was nice to others and had understanding and empathy, but I didn't have the same faith-driven principles instilled in me. Nevertheless, Christina and I got along well, and she would often tell me about her love for Jesus and how He changed her life. I didn't relate to that at that time, but I still cared about her and so I listened.

But just having Christina wasn't enough to battle everything happening in my life. The pressures of the popular cliques and the derogatory names I would often hear whispered about me when I walked down the hall led me to feeling isolated. By my senior year in high school, I'd had enough, and I started skipping. What should have been a proud and momentous time centered around finally graduating turned into counting down the days until I could be done with school and start the life I'd originally moved to Los Angeles to find.

I started hanging out with older girls in their twenties, who introduced me to the Hollywood nightlife.

After high school, Christina and I went our separate ways, yet we never lost touch. She enrolled in a Christian college and continued to attend her church group, while I moved in with a roommate and started looking for modeling and acting jobs. My bad experience in high school had put a damper on my love for school and classes. I'd given up, and I felt like I didn't need college—my only focus was to make it as an actress and model. I didn't even have a backup plan, because I was naive and unafraid.

I signed with a reputable and well-known agency famous for their high-profile models, but my extremely blunt agent made it loud and clear that even if I lost weight (which she wanted me to do), I could never do high fashion, and that I was only suited for lingerie and swimsuit work. That wasn't what I'd set out for, and I wanted the opportunity to do more. But my portion of the rent on the apartment was high, and I needed to make money. It's extremely expensive to live in LA, and I had no clue before setting out on my career how much I had to take in and make in order to just survive. As a result, I took on as many jobs as I could, from working as an extra on a TV show to waitressing. (Although I would always get fired in the first month—I found out I'm basically the world's worst waitress.)

Christina and I met up as often as our schedules allowed, and she always told me she was praying for me. While I was making bad decisions by hanging out with the wrong crowd, staying up late partying, and not taking care of myself, she never judged me. She didn't take part in my fast lifestyle, but we never stopped being friends. I thank God that she was there for me during this transient and unstable time in my life. She would ultimately be the one who would lead me to Jesus. Which was God looking out for me in a way: I had no idea the dangers that lay ahead in my pursuit to make it in the entertainment industry, because I had blinders on, and I was determined.

Although the modeling world may seem glamorous, there is a dark side, and it wasn't as fun as I thought it would be.

When I followed my dream and entered the real world of modeling and acting, signs started to appear that hinted I was on the wrong path. For instance, I'd be asked to pose "seductively," and though I never did anything too shameful, I'd leave the photo shoot feeling stripped of my dignity, like something wasn't right. I couldn't understand what was happening; I still wanted my dream, but my inner promptings were telling me that I didn't want them *this* way. The problem is, at the time I didn't see the alternative, so I ignored what I felt.

Photographers can be really manipulative. It's easier than you might think to end up with photos that, while not overtly sexual, can make a model feel used-up and stripped of self-worth. Every woman wants to hear that she's beautiful. Please don't underestimate the power of someone's words when they are telling you what you long to hear. I learned the hard way that my dream could be dangerous for me and for my soul.

> God speaks to our hearts when something isn't right. If we accept Him, His Holy Spirit lives within us urging us to do what pleases Him and not ourselves.
>
> —Nicole

God rescued me. Before I did anything I really regretted, He stepped into my life and made those conscience "pings" suddenly make sense. I finally realized this wasn't the way I wanted to be successful.

My conversion to Christianity wasn't an easy one. I'd become obsessively focused on my dream—to the point that I was missing the signs around me. When I didn't have God in my life, it was easier to keep moving forward with my worldly goals rather than to stop and change directions, so I kept doing what I felt I had to do to get the success I wanted. Inwardly, I was paying a price. In photo shoot after photo shoot, I was compromising my values by posing in bikinis. My breaking point came when I worked on a Taco Bell commercial and the director kept telling me I was not doing a good job. I felt anxious during the whole shoot, and I couldn't wait to get off set so I'd be free of the pressure to be perfect on camera. When I got in my car afterward, my tears came flowing down and I was a wreck. It was then I realized that I could no longer go down the path I was so focused on.

Depression was starting to set in, and I felt complete emptiness and regret for placing my identity in trying to be successful in Hollywood. Not knowing what else to do, I isolated myself in my room and started devouring self-help books. I would read two a week in order to forget my painful emotions, but no matter how much I read, the feelings never went away. It was at this time that Christina really showed what a great friend she was to me.

Then, in June of 2010, my beloved grandfather Roy died. Death has so much to teach us about life. I instinctively knew that my grandfather was in a better place. I understood he was in heaven where he was safe and not sick any longer, though that didn't fix my raw emotions. But his death did force me to start thinking more about eternity.

NICOLE'S TIP

You can't escape your emotions. At some point, they will catch up with you—either in a physical sense or a spiritual one. I pray that you ask God to help you with what you're going through, because only God can heal you. If you're avoiding unpleasant emotions, give them up to God and allow Him to speak to you through these hard times.

· · · ·

And we know that in all things God works for the good of those who love him, who have been called according to his purpose.

ROMANS 8:28

I missed Grandpa so much that it ached, and I started to talk to God more like He was my friend. This tragic loss really helped me build a relationship with God; as He says in the Bible, He can use our pain for good.

My prayers were pleading during that time. Each night, I would innocently ask God to kiss my grandfather goodnight for me. Truly, I came to God with the faith of a small child, and He answered by wrapping His arms around me and bringing me closer to Him.

I decided it was time for a fresh start in my life. The summer after my grandpa died, I made the decision to give my life to Jesus. I went to church for the first time I could remember, alongside my best friend, and my faith began to grow. Over the next few months, I worked hard to get healthy—taking better care of my body by eating well and getting good rest. I strengthened my mind by enrolling in school and getting good grades. I fed my spirit most of all by reading the Bible and praying a lot. I was becoming excited about life again. Now I just needed some stability. God would honor that cry as well.

I'd had so many setbacks in my life, but my grandfather's death was the catalyst for making the change once and for all. I knew now that life was more precious and I wanted answers from God. I wanted a purpose. I wanted to matter and feel His unconditional love.

After I gave my life to Jesus, the core of my being did not change just because I became a Christian. I still had the same personality. I still loved fashion, makeup, and being in the spotlight, but now my focus shifted. It wasn't just about me any longer, and I didn't want to do anything that made me feel compromised and not of Him. Now I wanted to please God. I needed to learn how I might use my gifts and my experiences in modeling for God's glory.

I spent the next few months learning about God and listening for what He wanted from me. As part of this, I started journaling in 2010 in what I call my "Miracle Journal," where I recorded my prayers hopes and dreams for my future. When I look back now, I see the seed of Project Inspired there in my journal as a dream for the future. It's so incredible to look back and see how God honored the musings of my heart. We think our little ramblings don't matter to God, but they really do. Writing down our heart's desires makes them tangible.

And then *ProjectInspired.com* came to be. I wanted to create a place Christian girls could go to and discuss everything that was important in their lives. I thought the Internet was lacking a place where teen girls could learn more about God and discuss boys and other teen issues like bullying, fashion, and friends from a Christian perspective. (Those issues aren't relevant to just Christians, but we are called to deal with them in a different and loving way.) I'm passionate about helping you to understand that your worth is in God and that He has a perfect purpose for your life that will bring you lasting fulfillment and contentment!

> *The LORD is close to the brokenhearted*
> *and saves those who are crushed in spirit.*
>
> PSALM 34:18

When you face difficult and trying times, I want you to understand that all of these challenges and hurdles can be used for God's glory to turn you into a stronger person. It's not always going to be easy, but if you can look forward when you're in the valley, it can really help change your attitude while times are tough. You're not "a bad Christian" because you've sinned, or you were depressed, or you've been bullied in school. God loves you unconditionally, and nothing can separate you from His unending, all-encompassing love. Trust me! The Bible tells us we are not exempt from struggles because of our beliefs.

One of the things I love most about Project Inspired is my weekly video chat, where I can talk to girls personally and get to know them. I also created a forum where girls can post their questions and share advice with each other on their individual struggles. My writers and I offer personal advice and tips to help teen girls in their own lives. I wish there had been a place like that when I was struggling, because I really had nowhere to turn during that time. God has truly blessed this dream—what started out as my inner desires and dreams turned into a blessing for not just me, but many others. I'm so honored that God chose to use me in this way.

And I am convinced that nothing can ever separate us from God's love. Neither death nor life, neither angels nor demons, neither our fears for today nor our worries about tomorrow—not even the powers of hell can separate us from God's love.

ROMANS 8:38 (NLT)

CHAPTER 2
TRUE BEAUTY & YOUR WARDROBE ESSENTIALS

TRUE BEAUTY & YOUR WARDROBE ESSENTIALS

I'm so grateful that I can now enjoy fashion on my own terms. Before, when I was modeling, I would often have to wear immodest clothing or pose in bikinis and lingerie, whether I wanted to or not, in order to keep working. And even if you've never been a model, the entertainment industry and the media have had an effect on you too. TV, movies, advertisements, and magazines tell us that we must dress scandalously and "show it all off" in order to be beautiful, or that we need to look provocative to attract a man. Almost everywhere we turn, celebrities and artists are wearing whatever it takes to get noticed, and as a result there's a real lack of clothing companies or public figures who show girls how to dress in a beautiful but tasteful manner. It's a shame, because our personal style is one of the many ways we get to express ourselves. The clothes we wear can represent the image *we* want to portray to the world around us. Personal style for me has been the way I get to tell my story and progression throughout my life. The way I dress continues to change and evolve, just as I do—right now, I would consider my personal style to be feminine and classic. But no matter what your style is, the important thing is that you feel your absolute best. You will never be comfortable with the clothes you put on if you're uncomfortable in your own skin, as our appearance should (and does) reflect who we are on the inside.

Women want to feel beautiful—it is perfectly natural. And it is a topic that is mentioned often in the Bible. Whether discussing Sarah, Queen Vashti, Queen Esther, or King David's beautiful daughter, Tamar, clearly there is nothing unbiblical about wanting to look your best. Inspired girls know that real beauty comes from within and emanates like a sparkling light out into the world. Our outer image, the one we project to the world, can help us build our confidence and boost our self-esteem. So as Christian girls, it's okay to want to feel pretty and at our best.

If fashion isn't your thing, that's fine. That's perfectly reasonable. Maybe you're an athlete by nature, or someone who prefers comfort over making a big statement every day. Whatever your fashion persona, however, I think you'll find these tips and tricks helpful in feeling more confident with your image. God created you to be you—be true to yourself in His image above all else!

Ever heard the expression "You can put lipstick on a pig, but it's still a pig"? You can wear the nicest makeup and most beautiful clothes in the world, but if your heart is cruel, it will take away from your outward beauty and you'll attract the wrong kind of people. The Bible is uncompromising in the belief that our inner beauty is far more important than anything we can put on our bodies, and uses a pig analogy as well: "Like a gold ring in a pig's snout is a beautiful woman who shows no discretion" (Proverbs 11:22).

QUEEN ESTHER: FASHIONISTA AND RESCUER OF HER PEOPLE

The book of Esther in the Bible tells the story of King Xerxes' search for a new queen. His plan revolved around holding the first recorded beauty pageant, where every young and beautiful virgin in his kingdom was brought before him in turn until he found "the one."

Every woman had to undergo a year of beauty treatments before she was even allowed to be seen by the king. Free spa days for everyone!

Why? Because these young women wanted to look and feel their best for the king.

(I love this story because I enjoy the idea that a year of spa treatments is biblical. Granted, my theological interpretation may be slightly off, but I'm going to go with it because I know I'm better for God when I'm at my best.)

The king's decree brought to his palace many beautiful young women, but none was more beautiful than Esther.
—Esther 2:9

It's important to understand that Esther carefully considered what she wore before she stepped in front of the king. When it came Esther's turn to be presented to the king, she was allowed to choose her attire, and she took the advice of the first stylist in history when she prepared herself: "She requested nothing but what Hegai the king's eunuch, the custodian of the women, advised. And Esther obtained favor in the sight of all who saw her"(Esther 2:15).

In other words, she listened to others' good advice and acted on it. It's great to get outside opinions when figuring out daily issues. And in this case, Esther's carefully considered choice impressed the king enough that he chose her to be his wife.

Later, Esther had to use her clothing choices again, this time for an important cause—saving the Jewish people.

On the third day Esther put on her royal robes and stood in the inner court of the palace, in front of the king's hall. The king was sitting on his royal throne in the hall, facing the entrance. When he saw Queen Esther standing in the court, he was pleased with her and held out to her the gold scepter that was in his hand. So Esther approached and touched the tip of the scepter.

ESTHER 5:1–2

I love that she has to dress in her royal robes. If you read the entire book of Esther, the king is so taken with her quiet beauty and respectful way of presenting herself, he grants her anything she wants.

Anything! And she had an outfit for each occasion. See what the right outfit can do for your self-confidence? You may not need to save an entire race of people, but maybe you need that new job!

GETTING STARTED: THE INSPIRED GIRL'S CLOSET ESSENTIALS

Every wardrobe, regardless of your individual style, must begin with the right foundation. As you build your wardrobe, remember not to become obsessed with trends. One year it's all about neon colors, and the next it's soft pastel shades—so have fun with fashion, but be sure to to focus on what you feel great in.

Styles will come and go, but having the basics will help you build your own individual look. With that in mind, here are some wardrobe essentials that every girl needs in her closet.

#1: A Nude Bra

Let's start at the beginning, shall we? I can't express how helpful it is to start your outfit with a well-fitting and flattering bra. Take the time and opportunity to get fitted so that you can determine your correct size. Many stores offer this service with no purchase necessary. After the fitting, you should feel more confident in the size and style that works best for you. Keep in mind that there is no price that guarantees a suitable bra for your body type. Bra prices range, and finding the right bra for you is priceless. Get a nude one that you can wear with everything, but make sure to try it on underneath a T-shirt, so you can make sure there are no obvious lines or bulges.

#2: Camisoles

Camisoles go with absolutely every outfit. I use my tan, white, and black camisoles all the time. They're helpful under sheer tops, work as a good layering piece, and are an inexpensive investment. I get mine from Forever 21 for about $5.50. You can't beat that!

#3: A Black or White T-Shirt

A plain T is so versatile and acts as the perfect foundation to any casual look. Tees are easy to wear because you can keep it casual for the day and simply change up the accessories for a night look. Black and white T-shirts pretty much go with everything—just keep color combinations in mind. Black can look a little harsh with certain colors such as orange and yellow, and you don't want to wash yourself out by pairing white with a lot of lighter tones. Use your T-shirts as pieces that showcase, but don't overshadow a great pair of pants or a statement necklace.

NICOLE'S TIP

I love the simple T-shirts from H&M. They carry them in almost every color, and they're usually under $10!

#4: Dark Denim

There are very few things in life that are guaranteed, but I can most certainly say that dark denim is a guaranteed essential in any girl's closet. Because a dark wash can be paired with almost anything, it will become a go-to item in your everyday life. If you are setting out to buy a new pair of dark-washed jeans, go for a boot cut, which is versatile and flattering on everyone.

If you love the comfort and convenience of jeans, you will be addicted to the endless other options of styles and colors as well. From skinny to flare, bright-colored to the ever-versatile black jeans, there is no doubt a pair out there for you.

If you find a pair of jeans that fit well but the price tag is a little too high, keep an eye out in the clearance section. Or head to stores like Nordstrom Rack, as often the jeans there are the same brands as the department stores, but they're discounted.

I also never buy jeans online. It's one of those pieces of clothing you have to try on to get the right fit. There are so many types of jeans to choose from, and depending on your body type, your favorite brands will vary. (I never buy shoes online either. See Online Shopping Tips later in the book for more info on what to buy in person versus online!)

Brands I Love for Jeans & Pants:

- J Brand (Come in extra-long length if you have long legs)
- Paige Denim (Super stretchy & comfortable)
- Kut from Los Angeles (Material is extra soft)
- The Limited (High-waisted jeans that are super flattering)

#5: A Great, Versatile Dress

One of my personal favorite things to wear is a dress! I feel glam and most like myself in feminine dresses. Whether it's a little black dress or a casual day dress, these wardrobe essentials can be worn in endless ways all year long. To get the most out of your dress, go for a solid color that flatters your shape and compliments your skin tone. By investing in a classic style, you can change it up by adding trendy statement pieces like jewelry and belts.

NICOLE'S TIP

Do some research before embarking on a dress hunt.
Research various styles like the fit and flare, A-line, sheath dress,
and more to discover what is best for your lifestyle and body type.
I've also included some information later in this chapter.

* * *

#6: A Great Jean Jacket

Another staple you should have in your closet is a jean jacket. You will get a ton of wear out of your jacket, since you can wear it with most of your casual outfits. Pick a style and wash you love, and start wearing it with your day dress and maxi skirts, or pair it with skinny black denim, a striped shirt, and cute booties. Comfortable and chic.

NICOLE'S TIP

In the warmer months, a cropped denim vest
is a fun way to rock this essential.
I'll show you more cute ways coming up!

* * *

#7: Black Flats

Who doesn't love comfortable flats? A classy pair can be worn with pants, jeans, skirts, and dresses. Every girl should own a pair that goes with everything! Find a style that works for you. Do you like a little embellishment on them? A little leopard print? Or maybe a pretty metallic accent, like gold? After you decide what you prefer, you can find black flats almost anywhere in the mall. If you want to invest in a good pair, head to a department store and look for a well-made flat that will last you a long time. You can easily find a pair under $30 as well. Try Forever 21 or Zara—they have really cute shoes there.

STYLING THE ESSENTIALS

Now that you have the basics, let's start styling them! Below, I show you how to wear some of the wardrobe essentials so you can see how many possibilities there are. I am focusing on the jean jacket, a plain back T-shirt, and a little black dress.

The Jean Jacket

Pair your jean jacket over a classic summer dress. A patterned dress is made even cuter by pairing it with a fitted jean jacket. (A fitted jacket is perfect to wear with dresses and skirts because it highlights the waist.) Keep the rest of the look fresh by wearing tan wedges, and add a splash of color through a bright purse. Bring the whole look together with a gold statement necklace, making this look effortless and chic.

NICOLE'S TIP

When shopping for a jean jacket, be sure to pick a style and wash that compliments your personal taste so you can get the most use out of it. If you plan to wear it mostly in the summer, maybe you want a light wash. If you want to wear it year-round, go for a darker shade.

Try a nautical look by wearing your jean jacket with a striped dress. For instance, a darker wash jacket looks great with a navy-striped dress!

NICOLE'S TIP

I prefer more of a cropped jean jacket, because it looks more polished over dresses with skirts.

A jean jacket was made for everyday outfits. This look is something I would wear while running errands. I started with my black skinny jeans, which I rolled up to create a laid-back look. I chose a graphic tee and my favorite booties and layered a light-wash jean jacket over it. Even though the jacket is not as fitted, it creates a balanced look, since my jeans are slimming. Last, I chose a cross-body bag, since it is ideal for a day when you need to be hands-free. This look is definitely comfortable for a day around town and is also stylish.

Jean Vest

A jean vest can be worn with basically everything a jean jacket can be worn with, just in the warmer months. To achieve this look, start with a classic silhouette like this A-line skirt and add color through a printed tee—chose a feminine floral. I then layered a jean vest over the tee. The length of this vest works well with the look because it ends just as the skirt begins, drawing attention to your waist. Since you'll be wearing this in the warmer months, go for an elongating nude wedge sandal.

If you can't see yourself in a jean jacket, there are still other ways to get the look. A chambray shirt is one good option, as it's a lightweight denim-inspired fabric that you can layer over a white camisole top in the summer. Wear your chambray shirt over jeans and add a girly touch by layering some gold necklaces.

Here, I paired a chambray shirt with a plain tee and brightened it up with colored denim. In this case, the coral denim compliments the light-blue chambray shirt, and long gold necklaces add a girly touch to the look. I finished my look with a tan-colored tote and some gray fringed booties.

NICOLE'S TIP
Tie a knot in your chambray shirt at your waist to give the look a casual and flattering shape.

• • •

Black T-Shirt

Your black tee is a staple piece in your closet. The trick to wearing it successfully is to build your look around it, not have it be the center of the outfit. For instance, you can use your black tee to create a polished and preppy look for the classroom. I tucked my shirt into a pair of gray skinny jeans and paired it with a heather gray cotton blazer that gives the outfit a collegiate look. I suggest wearing comfortable shoes like a sneaker or a cute flat, and go minimal with the accessories: a long necklace will keep this look casual but still very cute.

NICOLE'S TIP

Cuffing your jeans is a great way to make them more casual and also show off your shoes!

A black T-shirt is also one of the most versatile items you will own, because it really can go with anything. Use it as a foundation for a casual look by balancing it with darker shades. I love a good vest, and this military-inspired one works as the statement piece of my look. Dark-wash denim especially looks great with a plain black T, because it keeps the look balanced and is easy on the eye. I then chose brown tones as a neutral accent, opting for comfortable tan booties and a small cocoa-colored purse.

Don't be afraid to use your black T-shirt for an evening look as well. Pair it with a bright bottom, like this abstract floral-print skirt. (This skirt is a perfect length, as it hits right at the knee, making it modest and flattering.) Then add a pop of color through your shoes—and if you need to keep warm for the evening, be sure to grab a sleek extra layer, like a leather jacket. A gold necklace is the perfect finishing touch for this night-out look.

And this look can also be great for day as well. Just use a plain white T-shirt and opt for nude sandals or wedges.

Try an edgy look! Grab your black T-shirt and start layering your favorite tough-girl pieces. This look is all about mastering layering while using different shades of gray and black. The secret is that the black denim is a lighter wash than the black T-shirt, creating contrast, and the lighter gray of the boots complements the entire look by adding a neutral pop. A black faux-leather vest adds texture and is a simple way to create an edgy night-out look. Get a motorcycle-chic look by tucking your skinny jeans in your boots, showing the boots' details.

The Classic LBD

A great black dress is an essential in any girl's wardrobe, because one with a classic or timeless feel can be dressed up or dressed down depending on the season or the occasion. To me, the perfect version fits well, makes you feel comfortable, and is something you can wear to many different events. I suggest spending a bit more on this essential to make sure the quality and fit are better so that the dress lasts. Also take your time to find to find the right option for you. Is the fabric comfortable? Is it proportioned well for your body type?

For inspiration, here are some easy looks you can re-create with your own black dress.

Spring is a great time to add floral accents (or real flowers) to your look! I love the colors of this floral cardigan over my black dress. It is the perfect cropped length, flattering my waist. My brown wedges and gold necklace compliment this look perfectly, and make it great for a springtime brunch.

NICOLE'S TIP

Floral prints come in a variety of colors, so find a print that you like and incorporate similar colors into your look, like I did here with my brown wedges.

· · ·

Keep your style cool in the summer heat. A denim vest can go over any summer dress, including your black one! Keep the rest of the look casual with details like some strappy wedges, layered necklaces, and cute shades, and you are ready for a fun day in the sun. You could even wear this to a friend's graduation party and still feel dressed up if you decide to take off the denim vest.

NICOLE'S TIP

When your look is a little simpler, have fun with jewelry, like I did here with this pink statement necklace and matching bracelets.

• • • •

A little black dress is the perfect foundation for a layered fall look. Throw a knit zip-up sweater with metallic details on over your dress to give it a shirt-and-skirt look. Black tights and knee-length boots will keep your legs warm, in addition to making you appear taller! A beanie with a fun detail, such as a cute bow on the side, can be a functional accessory and the perfect finishing touch.

NICOLE'S TIP

Layering is easiest when you use similar colors, so play with textures and details to make your look interesting!

• • • •

The holidays call for festive outfits. Add sparkle to your little black dress with a crystal-embellished belt, a statement shoe such as red sequin pumps, and some fun costume jewelry. Be sure to bring a faux fur coat that adds texture and dresses up this holiday look. Now you are ready for a New Year's celebration!

NICOLE'S TIP

Red is a great color to add to your holiday look. Pair a red clutch or red lips to make your look pop!

• • •

I love the holidays because it's the time of year that you can really dress up, and there are more opportunities to go for a glamorous look. There's no better time to add sparkle, beads, and crystals to your outfit! Plus, adding rich jewel tones for the holidays is gorgeous on all skin colors. I especially love deep red, rich purple, and cobalt blue. If you only have one black dress that you love, accessorize it with different jewelry, shoes, and a bag or clutch. It just takes a little creativity to transform a simple black dress into something more dramatic.

I wore this dress for Christmas, and I like the detailed lace on top. During the shoot a fan wanted to take a picture with me!

MODESTY TIPS & TRICKS

No matter what we decide to wear, or how we decide to style it, one thing we should all be mindful of is the degree of modesty our clothing shows. Modesty means different things to different people, so feel free to adapt these guidelines to meet your own criteria for what modesty means to *you*.

Skirt/Short Length—For me, skirts and shorts should pass the fingertip test. I let my arms drop to the side of my torso to make sure the hem at least reaches the ends of my fingertips.

Dress Length—I recommend you bend over fully in the dressing room when trying on a dress. Make certain your bum is completely covered. Trust me, this isn't a test you want to take in public! Try before you buy.

Wearing White—Put your hand beneath the fabric. Can you see the color of your skin? If so, you may want to wear a white or tan camisole underneath that shirt or blouse. With shorts and pants? If I can see through them, I leave them in the store. No one but me really needs to know the color of my underwear.

Jeans—If you're wearing jeans, test for exposure by bending and sitting down in the dressing room. A comfortable fit is going to make the jeans work for you, and in turn will make you feel more confident. If all you're doing is pulling up your jeans or worrying how much of your backside others can see, the jeans are wearing you, not the other way around.

Undergarments—Invest in a bra very close to your skin tone, because that color will work under anything (a white bra can look neon under a black sweater—never a good look when our bra doubles as headlights). You also may want to consider a slip for your dresses. Buy a good pair of leggings to pair under tunic shirts and long sweaters. They are super comfortable and keep an outfit from looking too risqué.

Swimsuits—I love one pieces! They can still be pretty and fashionable without looking as though we're in our undergarments. I love two-piece tankinis too; they're awesome and allow for a bit more freedom of movement (especially if you're long-waisted) but still provide great coverage. Plus, you can buy the top and bottom in different sizes if your upper and lower body has different proportions.

CHAPTER 3

DEFINING YOUR LOOK & MUST-HAVE ACCESSORIES

Inspired Style Quiz

Style Your Shape: Different Body Types and Fashion Fixes

Shopping Tips

DEFINING YOUR LOOK & MUST-HAVE ACCESSORIES

Years ago, I was walking around a retail chain store that's known for its "hot" advertisements and skin-baring models. The manager of the store approached me and asked, "Are you a model?"

I was completely flattered, but now I realize that line is rarely followed by anything good.

"Do you want to work here?" he continued. "Because we're hiring."

I was young. With excitement, I took my first "real" job working for this store in the mall. It wasn't long before I started to notice my discomfort with the images that inundated me daily. I was surrounded by oversized posters of almost-naked, unblemished bodies that silently whispered to me. Was this the kind of modeling I even wanted to be doing? Even before I was a Christian, for me, I knew it was wrong.

At the store, the promise we were selling was unattainable. I started to look at myself differently in the mirror. (It wasn't hard with all those mirrors surrounding me!) I would see these airbrushed people on the walls, then I'd catch a glimpse of myself, and I couldn't help but compare.

Truth: When you're comparing yourself to an airbrushed image, there is no way to compete! It's not a level playing field.

While working there, I also realized how overtly sexual the company was. I would be cleaning the displays and organizing the clothes and be struck by the posters around me. All of them were of people making out with their shirts off, or were images of half-dressed models. It emphasized sex—as if this was the key to true joy and happiness.

Even the smell would lure you into the store's branding. The manager would have me literally douse the clothes in perfume and cologne—once an hour! Then, the next hour, they'd say, "Go spritz the clothes again."

I thought to myself, *Something in here stinks, and it's not the clothes.* It was the foundation of the company—marketing sex to young teens—that made me feel uncomfortable, and deep down, I knew it was wrong. I soon left the job. I didn't want to sell a lie any longer.

My experience at that clothing store made me realize how clothing companies really take advantage of young women by making them want to dress overtly sexual to get attention. I knew that was not my style, and I stopped buying clothes from that brand. After that job, I also worked in a few other retail stores and I loved it. Working with different brands and clothing stores gave me great experience, and really helped me realize how the right clothes can help someone's self-confidence, as well as let their unique personality shine through a great outfit. I have friends with different clothing styles, and it's fun for me to learn from them how to switch up my look and try something new and unexpected!

Have fun with fashion, and don't be afraid to be the best you can be. Embrace your natural gifts and let your light shine.

NICOLE'S TIP

*One great thing I love about fashion
is that as you grow and evolve
as a person, so can your style.
Be brave, and try something new!
You will learn to see things
from another point of view.*

• • •

I created this fun quiz on the next page to help give you an idea of what style you naturally gravitate toward, along with some tips to give you some ideas on incorporating new pieces in your wardrobe!

INSPIRED STYLE QUIZ

Who is your style inspiration?

A. Taylor Swift *(circled)*
B. Demi Lovato
C. Ashley Olson
D. Gabby Douglas
E. Nicole Weider

What style purse is your favorite?

A. A structured tote
B. A studded cross body *(circled)*
C. An oversized hobo
D. A colorful duffle bag
E. An embellished clutch

For a night out, your go-to outfit is …

A. A little black dress *(circled)*
B. Skinny jeans and a motorcycle jacket
C. A flowy skirt and jean jacket
D. A cute pair of jogger pants and a casual T
E. A sequin dress

You can be caught shopping at …

A. Gap *(circled)*
B. Forever 21
C. The local vintage store
D. Nike
E. Nordstrom

Your go-to nail polish color is usually …

A. Rich red *(circled)*
B. Midnight blue
C. A natural nude
D. Nail polish? Who has time for that?
E. A glittered shade

What is your favorite type of shoe?

A. Ballet flats
B. Motorcycle boots
C. A fringed bootie *(circled)*
D. Converse
E. A pink crystal heel

You get the most out of your …

A. Cardigan *(circled)*
B. Leather jacket
C. Cargo jacket
D. Zip-up hoodie
E. Faux fur coat

Your favorite accessory is …

A. A watch *(circled)*
B. A ton of stacked rings
C. A pair of oversized sunnies
D. Your fitness tracker bracelet
E. Anything that sparkles

Your friends would describe you as …

A. Timeless
B. A risk taker
C. Free spirited *(circled)*
D. Sporty
E. Chic

Unlock your style! Here's the key:

Mostly As: Classic
Mostly Bs: Edgy
Mostly Cs: Bohemian
Mostly Ds: Athletic/Sporty
Mostly Es: Feminine/Glam

Classic

You love sticking to the basics such as a great cardigan, a classic watch, and, generally, pieces that never go out of style. You gravitate toward the same group of colors that you know work well for you. Staying classy is your motto, and you probably tend to find things you like from Keds and the Gap. You're not usually worried about breaking any dress codes.

Tip: Step outside your comfort zone and try a new, bold color you don't already have in your closet. Who knows? Wearing a new color you love might give you more opportunities to create new outfits from your time-tested pieces.

Edgy

You aren't afraid to put yourself out there when you get dressed, and like things that make a big statement. Details such as metallic accents, buckles, or a bold print tend to make a piece of clothing better in your mind, especially if it comes in a darker color. You also tend to pick basic pieces with an unexpected shape, design, or a unique fabric.

Tip: Try things like lace-up boots, novelty tees, and distressed denim, as well as great statement items like a leather jacket, bold jewelry, or shoes with metallic accents.

Bohemian

You are a free spirit! You enjoy the outdoors and might be called adventurous. Maybe you've been called "quirky" or told you dance to the beat of your own drum. You tend to gravitate toward voluminous skirts and comfortable maxi dresses, as well as beaded jewelry, sundresses, and things that remind you of nature. This style often represents the artistic, creative types. Look for florals, fringe, a great basic maxi skirt you can wear often, long necklaces, and some cute ankle boots.

Tip: Try wearing an infinity scarf with your looks for a chic, layered look. Or if you want to be more daring, try a pair of leopard flats with one of your outfits. And for a touch of glam on a night out, have fun with a sparkle clutch! You can find these clutches almost anywhere— Forever 21, Francesca's, and Charlotte Russe have cute options.

Athletic/Sporty

You're always on the go, and tend to be involved in many activities. With your style, you might live in your Converse sneakers, see leggings as a staple, and buy anything that allows you to freely move around. You need clothing that keeps up with you! Look for fabrics that move easily and fit well, such as yoga pants (just make sure your backside is covered!), fun T-shirts, zip-up hoodies, fitted (not tight) sweatpants, or a great pair of skinny jeans.

Tip: If you want to go for a more feminine look, try a red or purple top with your jeans and sneakers. Those two colors look great against any skin tone. You can also try stacked bracelets to give your outfits a polished look— it's easy to find cute bracelets almost anywhere!

Feminine/Glam

You live for a good romantic flick and enjoy little details in your clothes and accessories. When you get dressed in the morning, you gravitate toward soft colors and generally love dresses and skirts. Your closet reflects your girly nature, and you probably love your florals and lace. Look for romantic fit and flare dresses, colorful tops, delicate accessories in gold or silver, and cute ballet flats.

Tip: To make your outfit stand out more, try a bold statement necklace over your top or dress, or layer a leather jacket over your dress. It gives your outfit some edge if you want to switch it up!

Even if you consider yourself mainly one of the above categories, it's fun to mix it up sometimes. Don't be afraid to try something new, or try on a new look for a special occasion. Enlarge your world! For instance, if you always dress edgy, try a day of the bohemian look for fun!

Although I enjoy wearing feminine dresses and skirts, I love mixing it up sometimes with a faux leather jacket or a vest, black jeans, and a military jacket. It's fun to switch it up, try new things, and get creative! After all, fashion is temporary; have fun with it!

. . . .

STYLE YOUR SHAPE: DIFFERENT BODY TYPES & FASHION FIXES

The female form, as beautiful as it is, comes in all sizes and shapes. Very few people are void of something they don't want to camouflage. Back in my modeling days, I saw that even supermodels get airbrushed—furthering the false thinking that there is such a thing as perfection. No matter what your personal style is, you will look best when you dress for your body type. And whether you are petite, tall, hourglass, athletic, slim, or curvy, there are a ton of ways to flatter your shape and highlight your best features.

If You Are Petite

If you're 5'4" or under and have smaller, balanced proportions all over, you fall in the petite category. To create an illusion of height and make sure your clothes flatter your body type, follow these tips:

Wear: Vertical lines that create a sense of length, solid colors, thin belts, tops that draw attention upward and add curves (such as ruffles, embroidery around neckline). Flare denim with wedges make your legs look longer (just make sure the pant legs don't hit the floor), and a high-waist skirt will bring peoples' eyes upward, which will make them think you seem taller as well.

Tip: Like with the skirt, a high-waist pair of jeans can really elongate your petite shape. Choose a dark wash that you can wear all year.

If You Are Tall

If you are 5'7" or taller, embrace your height. Sometimes you may feel a little self-conscious about being the tall one in the group. I know I was when I was younger, but as I got older, I "grew" to love my height. Here are some tips I picked up along the way.

Wear: Skinny jeans will really accentuate your long legs. Just make sure they're not too snug! Go for a high-waist style or a denim that has a long inseam that flatters your height. Since you probably have a longer torso, go for A-line styles and dresses that will hit you at your natural waist. If are on the leggy side, flats are probably your go-to item, but don't be afraid to wear heels. You can slowly introduce them into your wardrobe by wearing chunky-heeled booties.

Tip: Look for brands that have tall sizes, so that the garments are flattering and show off your natural height. Some brands that have tall sizes are the Limited, the Loft, and Old Navy.

If You Are Slim

Slim girls have hips and shoulders that are relatively the same width. And if you fall into this category, your bust and hips are also about the same size as well.

Wear: Your waist may not be as defined, so you may want to focus on ways you can create some curves and definition while highlighting your slim frame. If you want to create more curves, wear styles that bring attention to your waist and create shape. Peplum styles, empire dresses, and drop-waist tops and dresses will add dimension while still flattering your figure. Belted tops and dresses create a sense of balance and don't overwhelm your frame.

Tip: Adding a thin belt to your outfit will help call out your waist without taking up too much room on your torso.

If You Are Curvy

Curvy girls have a shapelier body with fuller hips, an ample bust line, and a waist that may be more defined and narrow in comparison to their upper and lower body. If you are curvy, you will want to create a well-balanced look that celebrates your female form.

Wear: Solid colors work best for you, whereas oversized prints and boxy shapes only add volume. Go for dresses that hug your waist and accentuate your curves. Asymmetrical styles also flatter and highlight your curvy shape and drape nicely over your lower half. Use accessories to bring attention to what you want to accentuate. A cute belt highlights your waist, while a great necklace brings attention upward to your beautiful face.

Tip: Monochromatic outfits are flattering, especially when they have draping or ruching features that highlight the smallest area on your body.

If You Have an Athletic Build

Athletic body types usually have broader shoulders, slim hips, and muscular legs and thighs. You work hard for your body! Here are some tips that look great for your shape:

Wear: Dark flared denim is perfect for streamlining your shape. Go for A-line skirts that balance muscular thighs and highlight well-toned legs. Tank dresses show your toned arms, but still give a feminine feel to your shape. If you want to create curves, wear dresses with details around the hip area.

Tip: Pick your favorite feature and highlight it. If you are really proud of your arms, go for a halter neckline that really highlights your shoulders and defined muscles.

If You Have an Hourglass Shape

If you have an hourglass shape, you will have a well-defined waist and your shoulders are hips will be aligned (the same width). You may also have a full bust. The goal here is to bring attention to the waist and highlight your natural curves in a flattering and classy way.

Wear: Focus on bringing attention to the smallest part of you, which is probably your waist. Wear dresses that gather or ruche at the waist, or wrap a belt at the narrowest part to compliment your figure. Scoop or V-neck lines flatter and minimize your bust line. Solid colors like navy, blacks, and tan emphasize your shape, as opposed to eye-popping patterns that may make you look bigger than you really are. A fitted dress works best on your figure and shows your natural, womanly shape.

Tip: Make sure to balance your look. If you choose a modest V-neck dress, make sure it falls at your knee to create a flattering appearance.

NICOLE'S TIP:

Need more inspiration? Find a celebrity or a fashion icon with a body type similar to yours and pay attention to what they wear and how it flatters their shape. You may also be a mix of these body types, or relate to one more than the others — the most important thing is to be comfortable and confident in whatever you wear!

• • •

If you are self-conscious about any part of your body (which you shouldn't be!), stay away from silk, jersey, and satin, which are fabrics that may cling to that part of your body. Those materials also aren't forgiving. I have a friend who hated her long, gangly arms, and she always wore at least 3/4 sleeves because she didn't feel comfortable letting people see her arms. If it sounds ridiculous, that's probably how you sound about your self-conscious area—but don't be afraid to camouflage something if you spend time thinking about it when you're in public. It's not worth the worry or distraction! Clothes should make you feel empowered and like the very best you. Use them to your full advantage.

SHOPPING TIPS

Now that you have some ideas of what you need to complete your own wardrobe, take these tips with you to the mall or when you shop online. The first and biggest thing to keep in mind: Don't try to accomplish too much in one day. Sometimes it's enough to look for one item to help complete your essentials list.

Look for a friendly face and ask for their unbiased opinion. If you're unsure of how something fits or you aren't sure whether to buy it or not, ask another customer what they think. I find most people are really honest because they don't want you to waste money any more than they want to waste money. They get it! Yes, you can ask the salesperson, but if they're working on commission, they may not tell you that, from behind, it looks like you're wearing your grandma's housecoat!

Take pictures in the dressing room. I'll admit to sometimes taking a quick picture of an outfit after I've tried it on. If the store staff only knew all that was going on in that dressing room, right? But I figure, better safe than sorry. The store doesn't want me bringing something back, and I'd rather not bring it back either. A picture is a great way to answer concerns when shopping alone, as seeing it on your phone screen will show you how the outfit looks in real life. Don't be shy, snap away! (And if you are shy, just mute your phone. No one will ever know but you!)

Spend your money on quality basics, then mix in some deals and steals. I LOVE discount shopping! Who doesn't enjoy a good bargain? It makes you feel like you've won something when you come home with a haul. (I know a lot of you actually Instagram your great finds so that your friends can appreciate your deals as well.) This is a great way to share the love and give your friends tips for where to find great bargains. My favorite place for discount shopping is Nordstrom Rack, but T.J. Maxx, Marshalls, and Ross have cute things too!

Remember when shopping that even if you don't buy anything, combing the racks and taking inventory of what's out there can be great fun. Even when the actual clothing is hit and miss—and many times, it is—you might discover how to create future looks or see an essential that you need to save up for to add to your wardrobe. The point is, it should be fun!

NICOLE'S TIP:

If you really like a particular discount store, ask them what day new shipments come in to better your chances for a steal.

• • •

Don't worry, be happy! Shopping is not rocket science. If it feels like rocket science, enlist a good friend and wait until they can go with you and offer their opinion. Afterward, treat her to a soda or Starbucks as a thank you.

Online Shopping Tips

Check for online promo codes. Sites sometimes have special codes or deals on the homepage of the site, so always do a quick check before you head to the cart checkout. I often check a store's Facebook page as well for any online promo codes that may not be updated on their website. And always visit the sale section first! Often they have cute items that are virtually seasonless. I've seen online clearance items on websites that are still full price in department stores. But keep in mind that many times when an item is on sale on a site, you can't return it if it doesn't fit. Always check the site's policy on sale items!

Know the length for appropriate dresses, skirts, and pants. I'm 5'10" and I need more length than average clothing comes in—at least 37 inches for dresses. Look for the length measurements on the website when you're browsing. The key is to know your measurements when buying online. You might be petite, short-waisted, or perhaps you want the shirt to be longer. Having the correct proportions to fit your body will make the outfit look better, and save fitting disappointments when the package arrives.

When in doubt, try the online sales representatives. If you have a question about a particular product, click the tab that says "Need help?" Online stores often hire really great sales people to help you with sizing and styling questions.

Find online shopping sites that show the clothes on a model or a mannequin. I find this makes it easier for me to visualize how something will look on me and where the waistline hits on a particular dress. This will also make it easier for you to see if a dress is too short or doesn't hang well, and will give you a better idea for what will work for your body type.

Fashion might not be the passion for you that it is for me and if not, that's perfectly fine! I just want to give you some of my best tips so you can use them to make the most of your wardrobe. Your clothes make you feel like the best possible you for what God has equipped you to do! (Sorry for the rhyme!)

Accessories

Having the right accessories can make or break an outfit. For instance, you can simply put on one awesome piece of jewelry and make your outfit stand out. It just takes a little creativity! Here are some of my favorite accessories that are versatile and a necessity in every girl's closet.

A Classic Bag

I love a classic black bag that can be worn for day or night. Look for simple shapes that will go with anything; I prefer a tote style because it is roomy and the shape is sophisticated and timeless. Or maybe just focus on a small detail that makes your bag super special. No matter what shape or size you prefer, you can buy a beautiful black bag at any price point. Check out T.J. Maxx for designer options.

A Scarf

A colorful or printed scarf can dress up any look. You can even tie one on the handles of your handbag as a fun way to bring a look together! And don't be afraid to wear a bold color or an interesting print. It could be a conversation piece, and it's an easy and affordable way to make an outfit more interesting.

Cute Bracelets

Silver and/or gold bangles can add polish to any outfit, even making an otherwise casual look a little more sophisticated. You can go simple or extra sparkly! (I prefer the latter!) A great store for accessories is Charming Charlie. I get a lot of my jewelry from there and it looks more expensive than it is! I love it.

This is how I display and organize my bracelets. I got this jewelry holder from Michael's, and it was under $20! I like to categorize my bracelets with like colors together, to keep them more organized and so my display looks better.

A Skinny Belt

A silver or black skinny belt always comes in handy as something to wear on top of dresses to accentuate your figure, and if it comes in one of those colors, you can wear it over almost anything.

A Great Pair of Sunglasses

Look for a black pair, and a little bit oversized. Throw them on for a chic look that adds an air of mystery. I'll tell you a secret—I buy most of my sunglasses at those kiosks in the mall! They look more expensive than $15, and they go with everything.

An oversized cocktail ring

It's something you can just throw on, and it makes you feel more glamorous! Who doesn't love that?

Faux Diamond Stud Earrings

A good, sparkly pair of faux diamond stud earrings is a must—crystal and cubic zirconia often look just like the real thing! No one will ever know the difference. It's an easy way to add sophistication to any outfit. You can find earrings like this virtually anywhere.

To keep my earrings paired together and easy to find, I put them in little jewelry bags. I only put two pairs in a bag to keep them from getting tangled.

CHAPTER 4

BEAUTY FAVORITES & SKINCARE SECRETS

Skincare Basics

Must-Haves for Hair Care

The Finishing Touches

BEAUTY FAVORITES & SKINCARE SECRETS

We only receive one body in this lifetime, and it's our job to care for it just like we would anything of important value. Skin is the biggest organ in our bodies and therefore one that requires a lot of attention. I hope these tips will help you to honor God by caring for the body he designed for you, and also make you feel better about how you present yourself in the world.

For instance, I have a Sunday-night ritual where I put a facemask on, apply a Bioré nose strip, tweeze my eyebrows, and apply self-tanner so I'm prepared for the week. Why not start your own routine? "Me" time is a great thing to start when you're young, because when you feel good, you look better, and that knowledge helps you exude confidence. Me time can also be "we" time, so why not get together with friends to encourage each other, and then apply an alien green facial and watch a movie? Talk about bonding! If you want to take girl time a little further, one of my favorite beauty treatments when I have the extra time is to put in a moisturizing hair mask and let it sit for fifteen minutes while covered with a plastic bag.

SKINCARE BASICS

When I was a teenager, I had acne. And it was not fun. Trust me when I say that I have seriously tried it all. It took several years of trial and error, and I probably tried hundreds of products. But thankfully, now I have clear skin, for the most part. Because of my experience, I want to save you time and money and offer you all the tips I know, so that you can get your skin looking as amazing as it can be! Taking care of one's skin is so important, and if you start now, your skin will be more preserved and look great when you're older.

I know you girls have heard this before, but one of the most important beauty rules to live by is to ALWAYS remove your makeup before you go to sleep. Even if you're tired, please wash it off! If your makeup stays on your skin while you sleep, it's clogging your pores and trapping oil. Makeup residue that hasn't been washed off your skin is one of the leading causes of breakouts!

Plus, if you don't wash everything off, you'll wake up with smeared makeup on your face, and who wants that? I always wash my makeup off entirely—even if I don't feel like it. I've endured the consequences. Learn from my mistakes.

My Easy Skincare Tips

Tip #1: I love e.l.f. makeup wipes! They are really affordable (about $3) and absolutely can take off all your stubborn makeup, including pesky waterproof mascara. I've been using them for years, and they are my favorite!

Tip #2: Change your pillowcase often! Even if you wash your face well each night, oils and skin cells get trapped in the fabric over time and can end up causing breakouts and irritation later.

Tip #3: Try not to touch your face all the time, or get in the habit of not touching it unless necessary, as the oil from your fingers can really wreak havoc.

Tip #4: Clean your cell phone often, so when you talk on it the oil doesn't get on your face. Plus, who doesn't like looking at a clean screen? You can just use a sanitizing wipe and, boom, you're done!

Tip #5: Exfoliate twice a week. This helps cell turnover and unclogs pores. At the same time, it will give your skin a radiant look and it will make the surface smoother.

Tip #6: When you cleanse your skin, make sure to clean behind your ears and along your hairline and jawbone, because you can get little breakouts there!

To Help Beat Acne

Acne can really play with our confidence levels. I recommend face washes that contain glycolic or salicylic acid—these ingredients really prevent breakouts.

I stay away from benzoyl peroxide. It's found in a lot of acne creams, but whenever I used it my face would get really red and irritated. It also dried out my skin. Instead, I've found that acne spot treatments with the ingredient sulfur are the best! Apply these products on only the acne mark. In two days, the blemish will be gone! A wonderful product that has sulfur acid is Nuance by Salma Hayak, which is sold at drugstores. I promise you'll love it!

Right now, I have combination skin. It could be dry one day, then oily the next. As a result, this list includes some of my favorite face washes, treatments, and moisturizers to deal with either oil or dryness, or a mix of both.

Some of my favorite acne products

- Look for products containing Vitamin A and glycolic acid. A really good face wash for your skin that also helps brighten your skin tone is Vitamin A Glycolic Cleanser by Derma E. Don't let the anti-aging thing scare you off, as it's fantastic for acne-prone skin. I've been using it for two years and it's one of my favorites!

- If you have a little bit more money to spend, I love the Peter Thomas Roth brand and Dr. Murad products. Peter Thomas Roth makes a great face wash called Glycolic Acid 3% Facial Wash that helps brighten, exfoliate, and even out your skin. It's $32, but the bottle is large, so it lasts a long time. The Dr. Murad face wash I love is called AHA/BHA Exfoliating Cleanser. This product has ingredients that really help beat acne!

- Derma E also sells an amazing exfoliating scrub called Exfoliating Scrub with Fruit Enzymes. This product brightens, cleans clogged pores, and sloughs off dead cells. I recommend using it once a week.

- The Zap Acne Treatment Device by Tanda helps diminish an acne pimple within twenty-four hours—it is a little more expensive, but it really reduces the redness and size of the blemish. This product is available at Sephora.

- Neutrogena makes an inexpensive face wash, which also exfoliates your skin to make it extra soft.

- Using a clay mask twice a week will help absorb oil. (When I use one, my skin looks especially bright the next day!)

- If you have really serious acne, please see a dermatologist rather than spending a lot of money on products in the drugstore. A prescription can really help get you on your way toward great skin within a short time. And since your skin health is very important, please invest if necessary and don't suffer with acne longer than you have to. It can cost as little as $50 to see a dermatologist, and you only need one appointment to obtain a prescription for a medicated acne cream.

To fade acne marks

One of my secret weapons and best-kept beauty secrets is the website *www.makeupartistschoice.com.* They have amazing face washes that help brighten skin and fade acne marks. Their micro polish has great exfoliating beads, which help wipe dead skin cells and lighten acne marks. You can even get inexpensive samples on their website. Also, I love their pumpkin exfoliating mask with 5% glycolic acid. It helps fade acne marks and prevents new blemishes from forming.

My Favorite Beauty Care Products

No matter what type of skin you have, or what products you use to wash your face, there are some other important steps and products you can use to really keep your skin healthy and protected from the elements. Here are some of the products I use and love.

Start protecting your skin from the sun now, so it stays healthy as you age. I can't emphasize this enough. A good sunscreen worn every day can prevent skin cancer, as well as keep wrinkles from showing up too early. If you have sensitive skin, a great product to try is EltaMD UV Clear Sunscreen. It doesn't clog pores, and it contains clear zinc oxide, so it's also the best sunscreen out there if you have a tendency to break out. As an added benefit, it helps reduce redness in your skin.

It's important to use a moisturizer as well. I love Neutrogena's Oil-Free Moisturizer because it's great for sensitive skin as it contains no fragrance. It's also oil-free and non-comedogenic, which means it won't block your pores! When buying a moisturizer in general, look for this list of ingredients in a skin-care product, because it means the product is healthier for your skin.

I use Aquaphor Lip Repair every night on my lips. It keeps them moisturized and healthy.

I wear Maybelline Instant Age Rewind Concealer at night, over my eye cream. Of course, you can wear it during the day as concealer. The ingredients in it, goji berries and haloxyl, help brighten your under eyes over time.

I adore the Queen Helene Mint Julep Masque. This product is designed for acne-prone skin, and helps absorb excess oils.

I use Crest White Strips once every six months to keep my teeth looking bright and healthy. Plus, they're easy to use, and I promise you they work.

Biorè Nose Strips really help to remove stubborn blackheads— I apply these once a week. The best part is that they're inexpensive and really do the trick.

If I'm having a particularly dry day, I use Evian facial mist to add moisture to my skin, and it gives me a glow.

MUST-HAVES FOR HAIR CARE

Next to our skin, our hair is one of the first things people may notice when they see us, and well-maintained hair is often a sign that we care about ourselves. As a result, I've put together some of my favorite products that will keep your hair healthy and beautiful, so you can always feel confident in your tresses.

My Favorite Hair Products

The first place to start is a good shampoo and conditioner that works with your hair's texture and type. I use John Frieda Root Awakening Shampoo and Conditioner—these products are really moisturizing and they're an amazing value. Best of all, they're available in most stores, so they're also easy to find.

For those days you're running late, a dry shampoo is a wonderful thing to have in the house. I love Dove's dry shampoo, because it's easy to use, and besides leaving your hair smelling fresh, it also gives your hair more body.

If you have hair like mine that sometimes needs a little extra oomph, I love John Frieda Root Awakening Strength Restoring Smoothing Lotion for smoothing out any stray hairs, and it also makes your hair extra shiny.

Every girl needs a good hair spray on hand. L'Oreal Paris Elnett Satin Hairspray Extra Strong Hold is amazing! It gives your hair more volume and holds your style exactly as you want it without being too heavy. L'Oreal makes this hair spray in a mini can as well, and I love the smaller size because I can easily toss it into my purse. That way, if I have a couple stray hairs I want to hold in place later in the day, I'm all set.

I love Philip B Maui Wowie Beach Mist. It's really volumizing and thickens your hair. After a shower, spray it in and scrunch your fingers through your hair to create a natural wave. It will seem like you have three times the amount of hair. I'm embarrassed to admit, I went through a bottle in one month! It's expensive, but I think it's worth it.

THE FINISHING TOUCHES

While caring for our skin and hair is super important, makeup and scents can be another great way to boost our confidence, or even show a little of our personality. Plus, makeup and fragrances can be just plain fun! Below I've listed some of the tried-and-true products and tools that can help show the best you to the world!

My Favorite Makeup Products

If there's anywhere to splurge in makeup, I believe it's your foundation. The wrong one can look cakey, clog pores, and make you break out. I use bareMinerals bareSkin Foundation, because it keeps skin clear and looks natural on my skin. BareMinerals seems expensive, but you literally use only two drops a day, so the bottle lasts a long time, making it a good investment for your skin. And because you use so little every day, it's actually as affordable as drugstore foundation. Remember, you can go cheap on lipstick, mascara, and blush. Invest in the right foundation—one that works well with your skin and doesn't cause breakouts. And if you buy your foundation from a department store, it can be great because you can try on several colors to get the perfect shade. My personal favorite is Sephora—I could get lost in there for hours!

If you like a powdered foundation, I love Mineral Fusion Pressed Powder Foundation, which I buy at Whole Foods. It's paraben-free and good for anyone with sensitive skin.

NYX Concealer is a great concealer that really helps cover up dark under-eye circles that are genetic or come from lack of sleep. It really helps brighten your eyes.

One of my favorite makeup items to wear is blush. I like that it enhances my cheekbones and gives my skin a rosy look. It wakes up my face on days I need it. One blush that I love is by e.l.f. I use the shade Candid Coral.

I love lip-glosses by L'Oreal—the colors are vibrant and they stay on throughout the day. The quality is great for the price.

NICOLE'S TIP:

An awesome website to check out makeup products, get skin care advice, and read and write product reviews is www.makeupalley.com. I have learned so many useful tips on there, and have found out about great products and had beauty questions answered. Plus, it's a lot of fun—you'll love it!

Lipsticks

When it comes to lipsticks, I love many different types. I love the brand MAC, however, because they're incredibly pigmented, and the color you see is the color you get. If you want to venture out and try a red lipstick, a great color is Lady Bug, which goes on sheer and is a flattering shade on all skin tones. Some of my other favorite shades by MAC are the colors Grande Dame, Sweetie, Dreaminess, and Creme Cup. Generally, when I choose lipsticks, I go for various shades of rosy pink. I notice this tone looks best with my skin color, hair, and eyes. Experiment and see what feels natural for you. MAC lipsticks are available at most department stores.

If department stores aren't for you, L'Oreal does a great job with their makeup, and that's the line I primarily buy from when I'm at the drugstore. Cover Girl also has nice colors. But again, every brand has some great items. Explore. Have fun with it!

Make Up For Ever Aqua Lip Liner in Shade 14C is one my makeup must-haves. I use this lip liner to fill my lips so that my lipstick lasts nearly all day. You may not think you need a liner, but once you use one, you'll see how much further your makeup goes! This color also looks good on just about any skin tone.

It's funny; women are usually either a lip-gloss or a lipstick kind of person. I almost always choose lipstick.

Doesn't it make you feel great to get a new lipstick or lip-gloss color? When you get the right shade, it can help brighten your complexion and give you a boost of confidence!

Eyes

A good mascara can open your eyes and make your lashes look defined yet natural. I use L'Oreal Double Extend Mascara—it's two-sided and comes with a primer you put on your lashes before you apply the actual mascara so they'll appear longer and lusher. It seriously makes eyelashes look twice as long and thick.

I apply liquid liner on my top lids only. The E.l.f. Black Liquid Eyeliner is great because the tip of it is fine, so you can make the line skinny or thick depending on how dramatic you want your eyes that day.

I recommend using a brown eyeliner—the brand doesn't matter. I apply it on the inner rim of my waterline. It helps me look more awake. You can also use your brown eyeliner to fill in your eyebrows if you want them to be thicker and not as sparse.

Eye shadow can both accentuate your eye color and add a pop of interest. The options in the L'Oreal Infallible Eye Shadow Collection are my favorite because they're very pigmented. The color also lasts all day and is shimmery. My favorite hues are Eternal Sunshine, Bronze Taupe, and Always Pearly Pink.

I also love MAC eye shadow in Soft Brown and Nylon. They are so versatile and blend well with other shades. I use them along my crease to make my brown eyes stand out more.

Tools

If you want to go beyond a simple swipe of eye shadow or a touch of lipstick from the tube, makeup brushes are a must-have. Some brushes can cost a fortune, but there are plenty of affordable options out there. Sonia Kushuk makes a really good, inexpensive line, which you can find at Target. E.l.f. eye shadow brushes are great quality as well, and I especially love their smudge brush and fluffy eye shadow blending brush. These smudge brushes are great for creative definition for your eyes. E.l.f. also makes great powder, bronzer, and blush brushes. I love e.l.f. in general because their price point is nearly always under five dollars, and for the money the quality is fantastic.

> **Makeup Tip:**
> Don't over pluck your eyebrows, because it's hard for them to grow back. Tweeze in between your eyebrows and don't go in too far!

Fragrance

Scent is such a personal thing, so I highly encourage you to try many different types to see which works best. If you want to experiment, Zara has quite a few scents that are under $20. You can't beat that! Perfumes also make great gifts if you want to get something nice for your friends. I often give Zara perfume bottles to girls on my video chats, and everyone seems to love them. Ulta also has a store brand that is really affordable, in addition to carrying other brands in all price ranges, making it a great place to shop for fragrance as well.

Fragrance Tip:
A small rollerball bottle can make even the most expensive fragrance affordable. Their smaller size also makes them great to keep in your handbag or backpack to refresh during the day.

Nail Polish

No matter what your personal style is—be it super glam or really casual—nail polish can be a nice finishing touch to any outfit you choose.

My everyday go-to nail polish color is a rich cherry red. It's a classic and goes with any outfit I wear. However, I do love experimenting with my nails and wearing fun designs with multiple colors. Nail designs can look like an accessory all by themselves! If you ever get tired of a color, or it doesn't look great on you, trade your nail polishes with friends to get different shades.

Remember, makeup is supposed to be fun. I believe it's truly an art, and our face is the canvas! It's also a learning process. Just within the last year, I got good enough to apply false lashes on myself! Practice, have fun with colors, and try something different.

NICOLE TIP:

As much time as you dedicate to looking beautiful on the outside, spend as much time keeping your soul focused on what's truly important, which is our relationship with God.

ETIQUETTE
A GUIDE FOR PROJECT INSPIRED GIRLS

How we carry ourselves and the way we act can also make a big impact on how others perceive us. I'm a strong believer in learning etiquette skills so that you feel at home in any number of different situations. If your neighborhood or community offers cotillion balls, sign up for one! It's a great way to learn how to act like a lady. Contrary to what modern culture may tell us, people still appreciate the refined manners of a genteel lady. If anything, its rarity makes such skills all the more desirable, and you stand out that much more. Think about it; would you rather have Miss Bingley's manners or Elizabeth Bennet's?

Here are some great habits to build:

Maintain a good posture! It sounds so simple, but did you know that posture affects the sound of your voice? It does! Speaking is one of the ways people decide who we are—our voice and mannerisms can tell so much about us in the span of one short sentence.

Walk tall! If you walk with purpose and keep your head up, it will improve your confidence level, and people will see you as being confident as well. Believe it or not, you're also less likely to be the victim of a crime if you walk confidently. Criminals look for easy targets who won't fight back, so appearing strong and organized helps a perpetrator know to move on to a different person.

Don't speak in a shrill voice. It's very off-putting, and you may find people stepping back when you open your mouth. Take your time when speaking and don't rush your words. Slow down the pace and you'll sound more confident.

Speak clearly. Don't slip over your consonants (i.e., brother vs. brothah) and be sure to control the volume of your voice. Getting the wrong kind of attention can be worse than no attention at all.

If you must chew gum, keep your mouth closed while you do. The same goes for eating. Just minding some simple etiquette rules and acting like a lady can help others see you in a more positive way.

Look people in the eyes when you're speaking with them. It lets them know you're confident in your words and actions. If this isn't something that comes naturally to you, practice. Anyone can learn eye contact.

Avoid curse words. They add nothing to your vocabulary and it's not remotely elegant. Why take the chance of offending someone and appearing uneducated?

Be kind. Listen carefully when someone else is talking and convey a genuine interest in what they're saying. Everyone longs to be validated, and this is a simple way to give someone else what he or she needs and desires. It takes so little effort. So many people are thinking about what they're going to say next rather than concentrating on the words of the other person. Be different and courteous. People will notice.

Mean it when you ask someone how he or she is. It shows you're authentically concerned for their well-being and that you care about them. Have you ever been asked how you were and then the person ignores the answer or speaks over you? It's a terrible feeling. Don't do it.

I'm also a really strong believer in not making fun of others. Don't laugh at another person or mock them in any way. It says far more about you than it does their faux pas. Kindness is the best etiquette of all.

Be free with nice compliments. I especially love complimenting older people who probably don't hear it as often. A simple "You look beautiful" can impact a person and make them feel good all day. Plus, what goes around comes around.

—Nicole

INSPIRED FOR ETERNITY

INSPIRED FOR ETERNITY: OUR SPIRITUAL GIFTS

Before we talk about how your gifts can help you in the real world, and how God has plans for your own dreams and desires, I want you to first think about your gifts and talents. You were designed with a purpose, and discovering that purpose will help set you on the right path to bring glory to Him.

This isn't about constant fun and the quest for never-ending happiness. (We won't get that on this side of heaven!) We all have to do things that we don't want to do in life, but ministry and your life's work shouldn't feel like we've just finished scrubbing the kitchen floor on our hands and knees. The majority of our outreach and our chosen career should utilize the gifts that come naturally to us.

WHAT ARE YOUR DREAMS? YOUR GIFTS AND TALENTS?

God has given us all gifts and dreams that work within our natural personality, so that we can give Him glory with our lives. It can be hard to assess our talents and spiritual gifts honestly on our own, but I'll bet that if you ask those who love you, they'll be able to help you understand the skills and passions you've been blessed with. Once you have a sense of what you like and are good at, you can take the important step of really analyzing your hopes and dreams for the future, so that you can fulfill your purpose.

Everyone has talents and gifts—areas that make us sparkle and spring to life. Ask yourself what you feel best doing. Do you like to run long distances? Do you love to write? Do you enjoy making videos or taking pictures? Do you feel at absolute peace when you're reading your Bible? Maybe you feel incredibly happy when you're creating hairstyles or singing. Just like with my experience, your innate gifts and talents won't change—you're simply refocusing them to give God glory.

Grab your journal or a piece of paper and take some time and write down ten activities you really love and that make you feel alive when you're doing them. What are you passionate about?

Now, look at what you wrote down and list positive results you have seen come from doing these activities. How have you affected other people's lives for the better by doing things you loved? Think about ways these gifts and talents might be used for God, as they absolutely can be.

Looking over your list of activities, take note of what they might say about you. God has equipped you with your own special talents, your unique abilities, and your gifts to the world. Take some time to look and pray over your list. Look for patterns that might give you insight into where your path might lead.

When we're working for God's glory, He wants us to feel alive and whole, like our entire being is humming because we're doing what we were born to do. With that in mind, can you think of how God used these natural talents in your past? Do they point you to a certain path or direction for your life?

As an example, if you love running, maybe there's a place in your town where you might help train kids from less fortunate circumstances, or help children learn the importance of physical fitness.

Maybe if you're an avid reader and love books, your library has a literacy program to help those who struggle with reading. Remember, what you choose doesn't necessarily have to be an official "ministry." You make it a ministry by bringing Jesus with you to the job.

When we use our gifts and talents to help others, we feel better about ourselves—more empowered and more alive—and that leads us to a more incredible journey with God.

For instance, I would say my gifts are leadership, encouragement, and faith. I love being a leader for girls who might not have an older Christian woman in their lives.

THE SPIRITUAL GIFTS

The Bible lists a series of gifts that are God-given and meant to help us further the kingdom of God. See if you recognize your own talents in any of these:

Giving	Service	Faith	Miracles
Leadership	Administration	Healing	Exhortation
Mercy	Apostleship	Helping	Tongues and Tongues Interpretation
Prophecy	Discernment	Knowledge	
			Wisdom

What If My Gift Seems Invisible?

We live in a world where everyone wants to be noticed. Each one of us wants to be validated and know our presence here on earth matters. When I say "be noticed," I don't mean compromising good traits in order to get worldly attention. Stand out by being a person of value and inner confidence who shines among those who don't have God in their heart. You don't have to be a celebrity to stand out. Be noticed for truth, godliness, and love. You will naturally become a leader and someone others want to emulate.

DISCERNING GOD'S VOICE FOR OUR PURPOSE

Sometimes we may know our God-given gifts and talents but have no idea how God wants us to use them. Don't give up. Don't feel worthless. God has a plan for you, and these topics and ideas can help you kick-start your amazing gifts.

Prayer—God answers prayers, so keep track of His answers (even if the answers are "no" or "not now," because you can look back and see Him working!) He will lead you to the right path. The Bible tells us again and again to pray and God will be faithful.

And I will do whatever you ask in my name,
so that the Father may be glorified in the Son.
You may ask me for anything in my name and I will do it.

JOHN 14:13–14

God completely answered my prayers when He delivered me from my depression. It's said that God gives three answers to prayer: yes, no, or wait. If He doesn't give you what you want, He may be blessing you by saying no or having you wait. I remember praying for jobs that I did not get, and now I am so grateful that I didn't get them. God was saving me, because He had something better to give me.

We don't have His perspective, so we can't know the reason something goes unanswered until the reasons are revealed to us—usually later on when we have received something more fantastic than we dreamed possible. When I was praying to be released from my depression, it didn't happen overnight. But I started learning more about God, reading my Bible regularly, and going to church. God's Word was a newfound spiritual home for me. When I prayed, I felt like I wasn't alone anymore. God wants us to be in constant communion with him.

Ask and it will be given to you;
seek and you will find;
knock and the door will be opened to you.

MATTHEW 7:7

Sometimes, God answers prayers by giving us specific steps or people in our lives to help us get out of our troublesome situation. Don't be stagnant when God is asking you to move. Below are some ways you can discover God is shaping your life.

Journal—When I first gave my life to God, I started journaling about my past experiences. It's been miraculous to look back and see how the tiny seeds He planted in my heart blossomed into God's will for my life. A journal can help you see that, over time, some desires don't leave us. They can also be the blueprint for our dreams. And you'll know something that comes up repeatedly may be from God if it lines up to biblical truths.

As you capture your thoughts on paper, see if you notice patterns in what you've written down. Are you being led in a certain direction? Is there some pressing desire that you can't shake?

Read your Bible—The Bible can reveal amazing things to you. Reading truth can reveal it like nothing else. When I stopped modeling and started reading the Bible, I was so overcome by emotion while immersed in the Word of God. When Jesus mentioned wiping away my sins, I felt loved in a way that I'd never known before. There is nothing like God's Word to make you feel embraced and truly loved, and see things in a new way.

> ## *In the beginning was the Word, and the Word was with God, and the Word was God.*
>
> *JOHN 1:1*

Look for "God Incidences"—I once read a book called *The Language of God* by Francis Collins, who is a former atheist. His book really spoke to me, showing how the book of Genesis and God's account of creation matches up with science. Around the time I read *The Language of God,* I had an encounter with atheists, who told me the Bible was made up and only uneducated people believed in God. As I was driving home one day, I got onto the wrong freeway on-ramp, and I felt a nudge to look at the truck in front of me. There, spelled out in big letters, was the word GENESIS. I realized then that God was giving me signs and I just needed to look out for them.

Are you seeing circumstances that repeat themselves in your life? Are you continually getting the same message from different places? These may be "God Incidences," so pay attention!

While the Genesis experience was amazing, for me, the biggest God incidence was when I was having an issue in my journalism class with a teacher. As I was praying before class started, asking for His guidance, of all things that could have happened, I felt the Holy Spirit telling me to look at the tag inside my jeans.

Why would God be telling me to look at my jeans' tag when I wanted an answer to this problem? Well, I was faithful and looked, and inside my jeans was this tag that read, "God loves you." I couldn't believe it. I'd never seen something biblical in a regular pair of jeans before and I haven't seen anything like it since. And I have to admit, I've looked at my tags a few times and nothing is there! What I discovered is that God reminds us daily in subtle ways how much He loves us, and He is in the small stuff.

Ask friends and family—We talked about this briefly at the start of the chapter, but it's a fact that sometimes we're too close to our situation to see our talents and gifts. Asking friends and family—people who love you for who you are—about the talents they see in you can be very helpful. Talk to people who know you intimately, and find out how they see you in the world. What do they think your talents are? Where do they see you serving? If nothing else, they may help you to rule out areas of ministry that aren't for you.

Connect with your pastor—Don't underestimate the leadership in your church. Maybe there's a youth pastor who has watched you grow up and can recommend goals and directions to follow based on how he's seen you interact with others or serve the church directly.

Sometimes, however, God speaks only to us. He doesn't share our dreams with others, and we must discern for ourselves when our path will take an alternative route. That can really make us question if we're actually hearing from God, but sometimes His ways are radical—like in the case of Noah in the Bible. The man was building a giant ark when there was no rain!

The gift of faith gives one the ability to see the Truth without seeing any evidence of it. Those who have tapped into this gift are a kind of visionary who can lead others to believe when hope is low. Corrie ten Boom was a Dutch Christian who, after helping many Jews escape the Holocaust, was imprisoned for her work. Think about how hopeless she must have felt being jailed for doing the right thing! Yet she said, "Never be afraid to trust an unknown future to a known God." She was blessed by God and went on to live to the age of ninety-one. That is the gift of faith at work.

We can't always see God's purpose in our struggles, but inwardly, we know we are following His will for our lives. Lasting fulfillment and peace is present in your work. You inspire others because you're being true to yourself, and because you are trusting God, He will direct your path. When I get worried that only I am hearing God's voice, I think about Noah, and remember that at least I don't have to build a giant ark in the middle of Los Angeles during a drought! I also realize that sometimes faith looks crazy.

It's possible you might consider yourself an evangelist. While we are all called through the "Great Commission" to tell the world about Jesus, those with the gift of evangelism are skilled in this naturally—and because they're comfortable witnessing to someone who needs Jesus, they are often pushed to do extraordinary things to spread the gospel as a messenger of God. Billy Graham is one of our best living examples of an evangelist. He has been traveling and evangelizing the Gospel since the early 1940s. He has spoken to millions of people, bringing many to Jesus with his famous crusades. Who knows what God might do with your gift?

Most people don't see themselves possessing the gift of miracles, but it may be a gift you have as well. Obviously, we don't see them all the time, but they are great examples of God's supernatural love for us, and great demonstrations of our faith. The gift of miracles is often seen in our prayer lives. For instance, when someone has the inability to physically get better and their doctors have given a dire prediction, you might pray for a miracle and see it come to fruition.

I hope that all of you have seen at least one miracle come to pass in your lifetime. Sometimes all it takes is looking for them and remembering what God has done for you! People with the gift of miracles have the ability to see beyond the earthly realm and see God at work. To me, Dr. Kent Brantly—a missionary doctor for Samaritan's Purse—has demonstrated the gift of miracles. Dr. Brantly worked with patients of the deadly Ebola virus in Liberia during a terrible outbreak. This is an incurable disease, yet when infected with it, he boldly said to Kent Smith, an elder at the South Central Alliance Churches in Fort Worth, Texas, "God's going to deliver me from this, but even if he doesn't, I have lived my life for him and I have no regrets."

He left space for God to work, and, miraculously, he was given an experimental drug that hadn't been tried yet on humans. He recovered, but truly, he saw a future that no one else could imagine. His recovery was impossible from an earthly perspective, yet he saw the gift of a miracle and received one. He then used his gift of healing to donate his new antibodies in his blood so that others could fight the disease as well. His belief in a miracle allowed God to work to save him and others who came after him.

No matter what your gift or where you feel your life leaning, you will know your dreams are God-given if they:

- Will honor Him.

- Will never go against God's commandments.

- Will bring us closer to Him, not farther away.

- May cause pain and be difficult, but you feel peace in your heart nonetheless.

- May be hard to understand, but the right attitude makes your journey fun and ultimately uplifting.

SPIRITUAL ROADBLOCKS

What If I Know What I'm Meant to Do, but I Keep Hitting Roadblocks?

It's hard to keep moving forward when we hit roadblocks. Sometimes, they're set up by God so that we take the alternative route that will benefit us long term. And sometimes they're just a frustrating series of circumstances meant to challenge us. Hopefully, either way, the experience will draw us closer to Him, and one day we will understand its purpose.

I Was Wrong about My Purpose, but So Was Saint Paul …

Think about Saint Paul. Paul—originally called Saul—knew Judaic law like the back of his hand. He was an Orthodox Pharisee from Tarsus—an intellectual who could argue the Law (Scripture) and hold his own with any scholar. Originally, he used that talent to persecute new believers in Jesus.

Imagine Saul's surprise when, on the road to Damascus, a brilliant light blinded him and Jesus Himself asked, "Saul! Saul! Why do you persecute me?"

"Who are you, Lord?" Saul asked.

"I am Jesus of Nazareth, whom you are persecuting," he replied.

Well, that would upset your world. You've been studying your whole life to be a perfect religious expert in this one area and a voice from heaven tells you that you've got it all wrong.

What was the point of all that study? Saul must have asked himself.

"What shall I do, Lord?" Saul asked. Imagine what he must have been thinking. *What now? I had a purpose and a use for all my skills, and now I have to abandon them all to follow You? I know what I'm talking about.*

Saul was so blinded by his own version of Scripture that Jesus needed to get his attention. And Saul wasn't the sort of person who got the message easily. He was, after all, the expert.

"Get up," the Lord said, "and go into Damascus. There you will be told all that you have been assigned to do."

Seriously? I was on my way to persecute more Christians and now I'm going to be one? Saul must have thought. *Uh, I don't think so.*

But Saul was physically blinded by the brilliance of the light God sent, so it's not like he had a choice. He was led to the city, where he met a respected man of the Christian faith, who told him, "The God of our fathers has chosen you to know his will and to see the Righteous One and to hear words from his mouth. You will be his witness to all men that you have seen and heard. And now what are you waiting for? Get up, be baptized, and wash your sins away calling on his name."

Then Saul was told to leave. Just like that.

I'm sure he was thinking, I'm going to use all this excellent Judaic knowledge to tell everyone about Jesus!

Only that's not what God wanted from him. God wanted Saul to go and speak to the other nations, when his whole life had been dedicated to being Jewish. And as Saul became Paul and began following God's plan for his life, God used him because of his infinite knowledge of Scripture, and his ability to preach it to the Gentiles and bring them to God. However, because as Saul he had just been relying on his own knowledge and not in trusting God, God had to wake him up and teach him that it was just as important to have faith in God along with his intellect.

Now, not all of us are going to be blinded and hear from a voice in the sky. That kind of clarity is hard to come by in this day and age. But I can tell you that my own "Road to Damascus" experience shook up all I knew. Maybe yours will as well.

Jesus should be a profound, life-changing experience in your life. He shakes up everything you believe and leads to a new life of using your skills for Him—not for your own gain.

We are not promised an easy path when we take God's route. Jesus said, "If anyone would come after me, let him deny himself and take up his cross and follow me. For whoever would save his life will lose it, but whoever loses his life for my sake will find it. For what will it profit a man if he gains the whole world and forfeits his soul? Or what shall a man give in return for his soul?" (Matthew 16:24–26).

Now, in hindsight, it seems so easy to understand that I wasn't supposed to model for my own glory. I was supposed to start *ProjectInspired.com* and tell others about my life-altering experience with Jesus. I was supposed to become a wife to my loving husband, Eric, and destined to be the mother to my darling Elijah. And I was supposed to become a Christian author. It's overwhelmingly amazing to think about how much better God's plan for my life turned out to be compared to my own.

Remember, Roadblocks Exist for a Reason

Sarah faced incredible roadblocks. In the book of Genesis, Sarah (originally called Sarai) has a dream. She wants to be a mother. She longs for a tiny baby in her arms. Not a spectacularly original dream for a woman, but Sarah has a special promise to help her dream come to fruition: God has told her husband, Abraham (who was originally called Abram), to "Look up at the heavens and count the stars—if indeed you can count them." Then He said to Abraham, "So shall your offspring be" (Genesis 15:5).

Abraham believed God. And so did Sarah. I mean, I'd be thinking, *I've so got this! God is so good! I want just one baby, and God promises my husband he will have, literally, too many children to count—like the twinkling stars in the dark sky! Woohoo!*

Then the years pass. There's no baby, and in Sarah's time that was quite shameful for a woman. I'm sure at this point Sarah thought God's promise sounded pretty bogus. I'm certain she thought that she must have misunderstood. *God said my husband was to have infinite descendants. Maybe He forgot His promise.*

Or maybe—and here's where it gets dangerous—maybe God just needs a little help to get started.

Have you ever thought God's timeline was slow? Did you once jump a roadblock erected to protect you?

Sarah had an Egyptian maid named Hagar. So, while feeling completely discouraged, Sarah concocted a plan. We don't have the actual conversation, but she probably said something like this to her husband: "Hey, Abraham. You remember how God said you were going to have all these kids?"

"Yes," Abraham probably answered warily.

Then in Genesis 16:2, Sarah lays everything out. "The Lord kept me from having children. Go, sleep with my maidservant; perhaps I can build a family through her."

At this point, Abraham was probably thinking, *Maybe Sarah is right. We don't actually have any children and I'm getting up there in age. We probably should find an alternative method ... But God did say ...* No matter what went through his head, however, Abraham does agree to Sarah's plan.

Years later, God did bring Sarah a child (Isaac), but by that point the damage was already done.

I don't know about you, but I wouldn't want to share my husband with another woman. And once Ishmael is born to Hagar, Sarah's troubles only get worse, because now, as the mother of Abraham's son, Hagar is attached to them for life.

God doesn't need our help to make His promises come true.

I know that waiting can be so hard, but now, in our present day, we still have the descendants of Hagar and Sarah battling it out to be first in our Father's eyes. Hagar's son, Ishmael, the father of Islam, versus Isaac, the father of Judaism and Christianity. The battle rages on—all because one person thought God forgot His promise.

Sarah couldn't wait, so she ignored that little rule about monogamy and paid a deep, dark price. We all did. Maybe your mistake seems innocuous. This won't hurt anyone. The truth is, when we push ahead with our own agenda rather than listening to the urgings of God, we will never experience the true joy that God has in store for us if we follow Him.

I also know what it feels like to act outside of God's plan, and I experienced the consequences to my actions when I hung out with bad influences, who negatively affected my life. Those bad decisions led to depression. I'm obviously not proud of those choices, but my husband always says, "Never let a crisis go to waste."

One of my favorite Bible verses, which really encourages me, is Romans 8:28: "And we know that in all things God works for the good of those who love him, who have been called according to his purpose."

That is so true. We're supposed to learn from our crises, not repeat them and let a previous lesson go to waste. Otherwise, we might have to learn it all over again. The Lord has washed my sins away, but I do wish I'd done things differently, even though I understand that God was using that route to bring me where I am today.

I want you to explore God's Word for yourself, so you can go forward with confidence in whatever God has in store for you. God will bless you if you trust Him and put Him first. If you don't believe me, put it to the test. Act on faith, believe God's promises, and take note of the results when you are faithful. When giving to the Lord, God told us to test Him here. He is storing up our treasures in heaven and He wants to multiply our good gifts for His glory.

Of course, there will be setbacks on our journey. There will be days when you wonder, What am I trying to do here? Maybe God hasn't called me to do this! I'm just going to hole up in my room and read other people's Instagram posts.

These valleys will pass. I promise. Experiencing trials is part of our growth. We are not in our final, perfect home yet, so we cannot expect earth to be heaven.

God has called you here in this place and time for a specific purpose, and I want you to know you are valuable, beautiful, and so loved by Him. He loves us to the ends of the universe and back. He only wants what is best for you and so do I.

But store up for yourselves treasures in heaven … For where your treasure is, there your heart will be also.

MATTHEW 6:20–21

We are all created with our unique personalities, natural talents, and special purposes in life. Just like the Bible mentions in 1 Corinthians 12:4–6, "There are different kinds of gifts, but the same Spirit distributes them. There are different kinds of service, but the same Lord. There are different kinds of working, but in all of them and in everyone it is the same God at work." The Bible mentions how each of us are needed for God's kingdom on earth, and that each of us are to encourage and lift up one another using our special gifts! Here are some ways that you can use your gifts to make the world around you a better place and demonstrate Christ's love to others.

- Volunteer at a local homeless shelter. You can also witness to them about Jesus while you're there. And who knows? You might save someone because of your kindness and generosity.

- Donate canned goods to your church during the holidays. Often Thanksgiving is a great time to get involved, as pantries are accepting donations for families who need help with their meals.

- Pack Christmas gifts for children without families. Your gift will really make the recipients feel special and loved.

- Send heartfelt letters to soldiers living abroad. Your letter will bring encouragement to them when they need it most.

This picture is of Matthews; he was able to buy kitchen supplies and a new mattress and blanket to sleep on.

- Donate old clothes to the Salvation Army. (I love this organization because it's Christian and they offer a lot of aid for people who are recovering from disasters.)

- Write a letter of encouragement to a friend. Your simple note will brighten their whole day, and that feeling can start a chain reaction. When they're happy, they can make other people feel happy.

- Visit a lonely elderly person in your neighborhood. They often feel isolated and alone. I know they would appreciate it.

- Bake an apple pie for a veteran or someone experiencing a tough time.

I sponsor children through the Christian organization World Vision. I love this organization because the money you donate goes directly to children and their families, and the people you sponsor send pictures of what they were able to buy with your generous gift. They also write you letters and send you photos of themselves! I have a photo album of all the pictures I've been sent, and it makes me so inspired and happy to see the children I've sponsored grow and see real evidence of how I was able to help them.

Living a life of grace and kindness is one of the best traits to have. Practice them, and I guarantee you'll inspire more people than you know.

This is Caren—with her gift that month, her family was able to buy a goat to provide milk and cheese to feed their household. They also bought various cooking supplies and clothing items.

FRIENDSHIPS & FUN ACTIVITIES

When I was a teen, I made some really questionable decisions when I came to how I chose my friends. That's why having such a dependable and faithful friend like Christina was such a blessing to me. She was loyal and prayed for me during the hard times in my life. Clearly, she had faith that God could do amazing things, because I couldn't see myself ever living her lifestyle at the time. Now I can look back and truly appreciate her faithfulness and the fact that she never judged me. She simply loved me and allowed God to work in my life.

After I became a Christian, I chose not to hang out with my partying friends while I grew in my faith and started to become who God wanted me to be. Hanging out with my previous friends was destructive for my soul. The truth is, once I stopped clubbing and partying, I had very little in common with these people. It's scary how shared bad behaviors can seem like friendship.

Make sure your friendships expand your world, bring you closer to God, and encourage you to be the best person you can be. You know your areas of weakness, so be wary of friendships that may, in the end, harm you. Here are some warning signs to watch for when hanging with friends:

Don't spend time with people who bring you down. People's constant negativity can deplete you of your own happiness. If you find you're emotionally or spiritually worn out after spending time with a certain person, limit your time with them.

Be wary of a friend who is constantly jealous of you. If a friend is jealous, they may not understand that when others win or have great things, it takes nothing away from them. This goes both ways, though. If you recently received something fantastic, be compassionate about sharing your good fortune. Don't try to rub it in someone's face if it's something they desired. Use your gifts and blessings to help your friends and inspire them as well.

Watch for friends who become too territorial. Territorial friends are probably taking too much of you and not giving enough back. Friendship must be mutual. Naturally, in any relationship, one person will give more than the other at a given time. However, if you find a friend is monopolizing your time and isolating you from others, that's not a healthy friendship. Talk to them about why they feel threatened by other friends in your life and let them know that you're capable of being their friend as well as other people's.

If a friend is too competitive, be careful. I'm sure you know of one person who is always trying to be the best at everything. Those people can be exhausting Whatever you do, they want to do it better, but this can be a waste of time for them and you. Friends should be comfortable with who they are and not be in competition with others. This kind of friendship can also be a distraction from building your own talents and gifts.

A friend who lies can't really be trusted. They may tell you one thing, but someone else another. If they tell a white lie to protect you from pain, that's one thing. Dishonesty is a deal breaker. You need to trust your friends.

If you find yourself changing who you are to be around someone, that's a warning sign! First off, no one can keep up "the act" forever, and you will either descend into that other person or you will live a lie. True friendship is based on authenticity. Be yourself.

Avoid associating with people who gossip. If a friend gossips about another person behind their back, chances are good that they'll gossip about you eventually.

Do not let any unwholesome talk come out of your mouths, but only what is helpful for building others up according to their needs, that it may benefit those who listen.

EPHESIANS 4:29

The root of gossip is negativity, judgment, and slander. The Bible also tells us:

A gossip betrays a confidence,
so avoid anyone who talks too much.

PROVERBS 20:19

And if you're someone who tends to gossip, try and remember this advice when you feel tempted to say something not so nice about another person. If you do have a moment of weakness, however, confess this as sin and ask Christ to forgive you. Then make a note to pray for change in this area.

No one should criticize another person. If you want to help them, gently tell them how you feel with love and respect. Criticism is never constructive when being said rudely or condescendingly.

Ask yourself, is your friend for you or against you? That very simple question will let you know if your friendship is true.

None of us is perfect, and we've all done this before, but it's a good reminder of how seriously God takes this sin. He writes so much about slander and gossip in the Bible that we don't have to look far to find yet another verse about the severity of this sin.

HOW TO BE A GOOD FRIEND

Before you can find great friends, you should know how to be a good friend. That doesn't mean everyone you befriend has to be a Christian, but here are some attributes to look for (and work on in yourself) that will help build and maintain solid friendships.

- **Love**—Have the capacity to love and be loved.
- **Peaceful**—Not a drama queen but instead a peacemaker.
- **Patient**—Listens and makes time for others.

- **Kind**—Goodness in their heart, cares about others.

- **Generous**—Is willing to give when a need is seen.

- **Faithful**—There for others even in hard times.

- **Gentleness**—Shows mercy and tries to understand others.

- **Self-Control**—Are in control of themselves and make good decisions.

But the fruit of the Spirit is love, joy, peace, forbearance, kindness, goodness, faithfulness, gentleness and self-control. Against such things there is no law.

GALATIANS 5:22–23

If someone has been a real friend to you, don't be a fair-weather friend to them. Encourage and strengthen them through the inevitable bumps in the road that we all run into.

Great friends are there for each other. Having compassion and simply supporting a friend who is experiencing a tough time shows great character in you.

Do you have a friend whose parents are going through a divorce? Have you been there for her rather than acting judgmental about something she cannot control? A good friend is there through all the seasons of life. They rejoice when times are good, and walk with you when times are tough.

Your friends will care what happens to you. Maybe you didn't make the cheerleading squad. A good friend will understand that this was important to you and will help lift your spirit when you face rejection or are feeling down.

HOW TO MAKE GOOD FRIENDS

Sometimes, whether because of a move, our own actions, or because a friend acted dishonorably, we're in a place where we need to find new friends. It can be a really dark, lonely place, but it's not the end of the world. All of us go through times of transition, and no one is immune from hard times—even people who seem to have it all together. If you find yourself in this type of situation, we have a great community on Project Inspired. You can reach out on our site and talk to other Christian girls like yourself.

Another good place to look for quality friends is at church. That is often the best place to find faithful people who share your love for Jesus and a desire to live a godly life. If your church has very few people your age, check out Christian clubs at your school or in your city. Maybe a nearby church has a weekly youth group that you might attend while still going to your own church on Sunday. Don't be afraid to step out of your comfort zone. You are worthy! Who wouldn't want to be your friend?

Also try extracurricular groups in your area where you might meet people who have a shared interest. A writing group? Maybe a photography club? The important thing is knowing who you are while you're looking for a friend. If that takes some discovery, take your time! Pray. Ask for guidance. Stand for God and be a girl of righteousness. It's inspiring to those around you.

KNOWING WHEN IT'S OVER WITH A FRIEND

Friendships go through seasons, so what might seem insurmountable may only be a rough patch, and you and your friend simply need some distance. However, if you've given this friend chances and told them what you need changed so that you can trust them again, and they don't want to change, then it's time to move on from your friend.

You can still be acquaintances and care for that person, but trusting them probably isn't in your best interest. God wants us to be around people who lift up His name and show godly attributes. Tell your friend that the relationship isn't working for you any longer and that maybe it's best if you spend more time apart.

Use all the extra time you may have to develop new, healthier relationships with people who return your idea of loyalty, instead of avoiding a conversation and hanging out with a destructive friend.

Remember, the only person you can change is you. You can guide someone to treat you with respect, but only God can change that person.

WHAT TO DO WHEN A FRIEND NO LONGER WANTS TO HANG OUT AND YOU DON'T KNOW WHY

By all means, ask your friend—in person—if you've upset them in some way. It's always better to speak in person when dealing with issues like this. Words can be misconstrued or interpreted in the wrong way when communicating over text or email. If you get the cold shoulder after speaking to your friend, just pray about anything you may have done, ask for forgiveness from God, and then let it go. It's tough when there's no closure, but respect the other person's wishes and move on as best you can.

Bear with each other and
forgive one another if any of you
has a grievance against someone.
Forgive as the Lord forgave you.
COLOSSIANS 3:13

DEALING WITH CHRISTIAN MEAN GIRLS

Sometimes cliques can be formed within our church groups, which is not only painful for us but also painful to God, who wants harmony in His church. Maybe these cliques are based on the schools you all go to, or maybe they are based on what style of clothes people wear or even what part of town they live in. Even if you're a Christian, you're not immune to bad behavior.

There will always be people who lift themselves up by tearing others down, or are threatened by others' successes. I know it may not feel like it, especially in church, but this is a growth opportunity for us. Christ loves you for who you are. He is grieved that these kinds of divisions happen in His church and in His Name, but He also allows us free will. Anyone can pretend and present a false image, but God knows our hearts and that is what He is concerned with. While we cannot judge, we can notice an absence of kindness and steer clear of that behavior in other people. Practice redirecting conversations that start to become negative. It's great practice and can change the energy of a conversation. People are drawn to positivity; practice it.

> *Be ready to do whatever is good,*
> *to slander no one, to be peaceable and considerate,*
> *and always to be gentle toward everyone.*
>
> *TITUS 3:1–2*

If you've been confronted with Christian "mean girls" or if people who once used to be your friends are turning on you, it can be really painful.

Many times the manner in which girls will go about this is to be silent—maybe exclude you from topics of conversation, or worse yet talk about you in the corner of the room, and then make you feel paranoid if you question them about their conversation.

The important thing is to own the truth. If people are treating you unkindly, you don't have to justify it to anyone else. You can excuse yourself from the situation. I know it's better to work it out, but that isn't always possible if someone hurts you in a big way. Pray through this situation and ask God what He wants you to learn from it.

Just remember, it really may not be anything you did. I think as Christians, we take all the blame for something that really may not be our fault.

Think about staying above the fray and not allowing yourself to seek revenge when you've been wronged.

> *Do not take revenge, my dear friends,*
> *"It is mine to avenge; I will repay," says the Lord.*
>
> *ROMANS 12:19*

We eventually reap what we sow, so bad behavior will not go unnoticed.

BE CAREFUL NOT TO JUDGE OTHERS

Sometimes, without meaning to, we can start to look down on someone who dresses a little differently, has different habits, or even values different things than we do. For example, maybe there's a girl at church or school who wears too much makeup or perhaps wears tops that are too low.

The Bible tells us not to judge, and the truth is we have no idea where someone is coming from or what his or her story might be. Maybe their shirt is too low because their mother taught them it was okay to dress that way. For the sake of argument, give someone the benefit of the doubt before you judge, and offer compassion first.

Do not judge, or you too will be judged.
For in the same way you judge others, you will be judged
and with the measure you use, it will be measured to you.

MATTHEW 7:1–2

I know there can be a fine balance between genuinely wanting to help someone and judging them. If a good friend is wearing something inappropriate, of course you want to tell them to prevent them from ridicule and unwanted attention from guys. Maybe their actions are bringing about gossip and it hurts you to hear it. Remember, always say things with grace and kindness.

God comes to people at different stages in life. The best thing you can do for a friend with questionable behavior is to remind them of God's love for them and be there.

Even if you have one great friend, treasure that person. It's not the number of our friends that we have, but the quality of people we surround ourselves with.

FIFTEEN FUN ACTIVITIES TO DO WITH FRIENDS

It's important to take a break from technology, which can take over our lives and get in the way of deeper friendships. With that in mind, here's a list of activities to do:

#1 Host a Clothing Swap Party! Gather all the clothes and accessories that you don't want or wear any longer and have friends do the same. Swap things—or if you don't want to permanently let something go, trade and borrow each other's things for a while. Try on outfits with different accessories and get advice or offer it. It's quality time with your friends, and you're guaranteed to laugh!

#2 Design a Dream Board! Go to a craft store and buy poster board. Then, cut out pictures from magazines and catalogs to create your dream life on the paper. This can really help you picture where you want to go in the future and what you want to accomplish.

Inspiring words cut out and applied to something we see every day can really help motivate us. It's great to share dreams with our friends as well. It will also make a pretty decoration to hang in your room!

#3 Closet Organization Day! You can have fun listening to great music while organizing your clothes. I organize my clothes by seasons, keeping the winter clothes and sweaters separate from the summer and spring items. (Short-sleeved shirts are grouped with other short-sleeves, vests are together, etc.) Think about organizing like items by color from white to black. It will help make your morning go so much smoother! You might discover new outfit combinations, or you might discover a clothing item that you forgot you had.

#4 Manicure Fun! Grab your favorite nail polish and experiment with nail designs. I like to go on Pinterest to look at fun designs and get ideas that way. It helps you practice your own skills, and when you're done with your friend's nails, she can practice on you. You'll both have pretty hands, which are an accessory on their own.

#5 Bowling at Your Local Lanes! It's affordable, fun, and I guarantee you will laugh! Even if you're not the greatest bowler. My ball always goes in the gutter, but I still have fun with my friends when we're there. It's also a great family activity!

#6 Create Some Crafts! Crafting is an amazing way to spend time together, and it's a great activity right before a holiday. Take a shopping trip to a craft store, such as Michael's, and pick out your supplies together. You can make picture frames, jewelry, fancy flip-flops, headbands, and home décor with a few beads, supplies, and a glue gun. My friend Amy is really crafty, and she decorated a few vases in her room with gold spray paint and it made them look more glamorous on top of her shelf.

#7 Trivia & Game Day! One of my favorite games is Catchphrase, but other fun games sure to entertain are Trivial Pursuit, Charades, or age-old favorites like Scrabble and Monopoly. For our last Thanksgiving, my family and I played Monopoly, and it was so much fun!

#8 Make Your Own Beauty Scrub! Brown sugar mixed with healthy essential oils is awesome for your skin. Plus, you and your friend can put the concoction into little jars, wrap them with a ribbon, and give them as gifts to other friends and your families. Name your product and decorate with special words you'd use to describe your loved one, such as *beautiful* or *precious*, etc.

#9 Old Movie Night! Classic Hollywood movies and popcorn—it doesn't get much better than that! It's fun to see what movies used to be. In my opinion, movies back then were more wholesome than today. My Favorites: *Sunset Boulevard, The Gold Rush, Gone with the Wind, Roman Holiday, Breakfast at Tiffany's.*

#10 Scrapbooking! Together with your friend(s), print out your favorite photos and design a beautiful scrapbook. You can go to the craft store and stock up on stickers, sparkles, ribbons, and other things to decorate your scrapbook. There are many sites that allow you do this online as well, such as *Shutterfly.com.* But it's more fun to print out the pictures so you have something tangible to see and reflect upon. No matter what method you use, make sure you arrange the pictures so that people can enjoy them and see a part of your life. It's really fun to have little time capsules contained within a book to look back on and cherish, not to mention share with others. Create them with friends, and you'll relive the memories while scrapbooking them.

#11 Sports! You can go on a hike with a friend to somewhere beautiful, or head out to someplace you've always wanted to go and never tried. Or you can go on a fun bike ride, or play basketball or any favorite sport. It's so much fun to arrange a day and a meeting place so that all your friends can join you. People are always looking for something to do, and getting outside together is a refreshing break from technology and a way to get physical!

#12 Marathon Day of a Favorite Series! Pick a show you both like, such as a classic like *Full House,* and spend a rainy day inside with your BFF and a few snacks.

#13 Makeovers, Selfies, and Funny Videos! I personally love funny cat videos. They can be so cute and hilarious. But if you don't have a goofy pet who could be the next YouTube star, get outside your comfort zone and create a wild makeup look—maybe copy some makeup fashions from another decade for fun, like the Disco era! Take pictures and videos and play them back for your own entertainment. You don't have to post anything online; the goal is to have fun with it! Another idea, if you don't want to tape anything, is to read some fan fiction together about your favorite band, or write one of your own! Reminder: Don't post anything publicly or upload anything your friend doesn't want posted, even to friends.

#14 Go Explore Your City and Take Pictures of What You Find. It's fun to be a tourist in your own town. That way, you'll have things to share with other people when they come to visit.

#15 Bake Something! Go on Pinterest and find some fun, easy recipes that you can share and learn together. Maybe you can make One Direction cupcakes!

There is no end to ideas that you and your friends can come up with for fun. I know you girls, and you're so creative! It's so easy to just sit behind a computer all day, but nothing beats quality friend time and face-to-face contact. These are just a few ideas to get you started, but come to *ProjectInspired.com* and share your own ideas. I know you and your friends have a million activities that you love to do together. Bonding is such an important part of friendship, and these are just a few ideas to create lifelong memories between you and your girls!

CHAPTER 7
NAVIGATING ENTERTAINMENT

If It's Not Encouraging Your Spirit, Is It Really Worth It?

Focusing on the Right Role Models and Protecting Our Sensibilities

NAVIGATING ENTERTAINMENT

It's hard to believe that at the advent of television, Lucy and Ricky—a married couple on the show *I Love Lucy*—weren't even allowed to be shown in the same bed! Instead, they slept in separate twin beds.

When Lucy was pregnant (in reality as well as on the show), she was not allowed to use the word "pregnant," and they had to refer to her as "expecting," which was thought to be in better taste.

Fast-forward to today's television shows, where the "Fantasy Suite" on *The Bachelor* reality series is part of the storyline. Where the Duggar family, with their sweet devotion to Jesus and purity before marriage, is seen as outlandish, and Christians on *Duck Dynasty* are constantly blasted for stating their views. We've become desensitized to the darkness in our entertainment and unaware of how far from the Lord's will we've gotten.

Even before we got to this point, wholesome shows slowly became less wholesome. *Full House* is one of my favorites, but the single father on that show, Danny Tanner, had a long-time girlfriend named Vicky. He never married her, and the lack of commitment was never seen as an issue. It doesn't sound like a big issue in this day and age, but the slow decline of what is culturally acceptable on television didn't happen overnight. It took baby steps.

Even the magazines have declined. Believe it or not, they used to teach women how to be a proper lady and gave etiquette tips. They were family-oriented and placed emphasis on a woman's worth, not in her sex appeal. I used to collect vintage magazines, and in one issue from 1898 there was an article talking about how to be a great wife like Martha Washington. Now it's more like, "Which hottie can you pick up in the bar?" There also used to be beautiful illustrations of the women in the ads, very much unlike the airbrushed, altered images we encounter today.

Today, in magazines, in movies, and on television, it's assumed that 99 percent of the time the couple is having sex before they're married. It's never a big deal to the characters, but they're reading from a script. They're not living through the heartbreak that is the reality of sex outside marriage. Of waiting by the phone for your true love to call, only to discover he's done with you. The script doesn't show the crying jags and devastating feelings of worthlessness that can be the reality. Or even if it does, the actors are paid to portray those emotions, and they'll be over it when the director yells, "Cut!" So while it's fun to watch romantic movies or giggle with your friends over a chick flick, if you start basing your future relationships off these fabricated stories, you'll set yourself up for disappointment.

Just keep in mind, when you're inundated with these types of images again and again, it becomes your new normal. You don't want an ungodly way to become normal for you. It's not normal to give your body away.

The sexualization of music has also gotten terrible. Nearly every pop song, whether sung by a male or a female, is about sex. Doesn't anyone write a love song anymore? I remember one time when I was shopping at a drugstore, and the music they were playing was an explicitly sexual song by Rhianna. I remember thinking that little kids are in here with their parents and they should not be hearing the word "sex" over and over again when on a family shopping trip. Later, I found that song playing in my head the rest of the day.

NICOLE'S TIP:

*I recommend going through your music playlist or iTunes account
and seeing if there are any songs that send a bad message.
Song lyrics can stay with you for a long time.
Pray about it and remove what doesn't honor God.*

As a result, when you hear a song that's about love or marriage, it truly stands out. That's why, in my opinion, Christian music is a safe haven that helps us focus on all that's right in the world. When we fill our minds with the positive, it's easier to leave the ugly parts of the world and focus on our eternal future.

My favorite Christian band is Newsboys. I heard them perform live in Florida, and I started tearing up when they sang the song "Your Love Never Fails." I love "God Is Not Dead," "In the Hands of God," and "Save your Life." Another Christian artist I love is Brandon Heath. His song "Leaving Eden" moves me so much. So does a song by Philips, Craig, and Dean called "Revelation Song." That one gives me goose bumps every time I hear it! God is so good!

I pray more standout hits that honor God will come our way and show real love versus the cheap copy Hollywood often glorifies.

On the topic of movies, I have a personal experience with the darkness that horror movies can bring. I didn't see the harm in watching scary films when I was younger. It was exciting and fun to get scared. But once you've given a place in your mind to those dark images, it's nearly impossible to fully erase them. Even as a child, the scary movies that I saw really affected me.

Looking at demonic things and/or making a game of the supernatural realm can really disturb your spirit. You're allowing darkness into a place that should be occupied with goodness and light, and that isn't healthy.

For what do righteousness and
wickedness have in common?
Or what fellowship can light have with darkness?

2 CORINTHIANS 6:14

To me, having these evil pictures in my mind isn't worth two hours of "enjoyment." I'm very susceptible to images. You might be more susceptible to the lyrics you hear in a song or the airbrushed photos on the walls. The important thing to note is that we are affected by the world around us. Know your weaknesses and take action to protect yourself from media that harms your spirit and doesn't bring you closer to God.

We are becoming immune to the fact that the dark, supernatural realm is very real. Even the way the supernatural is portrayed on the television screen has changed. There used to be a sitcom called *Bewitched* that focused on a "good" witch named Samantha who gave up her powers to be married to a mortal, Darrin Stevens. It was a sitcom that made light of "magic" forces. It was controversial back then, but it did focus on the timeless nature of good versus evil, and Samantha was a sweet wife who tried to do the right thing by staying away from magic so that she could love her "mortal" husband, Darrin. Compare that to how the supernatural is portrayed on television now.

Today, our television is inundated with the portrayal of true evil as heroic. Covens of witches and those casting dark spells to vie for power are actually the heroes of many shows on today. Books and movies also reflect today's fascination with the very real dark realms.

Please be wary of what comes into your homes and your soul. The decline in entertainment has happened so slowly, we aren't even aware of how far we've fallen due to our desensitization. The Bible speaks of how a little yeast leavens the bread. A small amount is all it takes to have a big effect on the dough. That's how a "little" sin is; if you let it inside, it affects your whole body. As a result, you want to be cautious about your entertainment choices and what you allow inside. Sin can slowly and easily become our new normal because we start looking around us and comparing, rather than looking up to the true Measure.

IF IT'S NOT ENCOURAGING YOUR SPIRIT, IS IT REALLY WORTH IT?

As children of God, we want to focus on what is pure and lovely. It puts life in a more beautiful frame when we protect our minds. Especially "entertainment" that features demons or exorcisms. These things are real. To take these kind of dark spirits lightly or dabble in the dark world for "fun" is to play with fire. We're told to have nothing to do with dark spirits:

> *For our struggle is not against flesh and blood, but against the rulers, against the authorities, against the powers of this dark world, against the spiritual forces of evil in the heavenly realms.*
>
> EPHESIANS 6:12

The more we pull away from wholesome, sweet entertainment, the easier it becomes to get desensitized to sex outside marriage and the dark spiritual realm. It becomes harder to have good morals when everything surrounding us is debauchery. I know that sounds very sermon-like, but I only tell you these things because they are true and I've seen the results of letting these shows, movies, and other media become part of your world.

Yes, it takes some looking around and searching, but there are good songs and magazines out there. You might simply need to take the time to weed out the garbage in your diet. For instance, when you get rid of sugar in your food, though you will struggle at first, eventually you stop missing it. You find your body is running better than ever. It's the same for our entertainment—what we put into our body is what we get out of it. If we put sin and debauchery in as entertainment, you can bet it becomes more commonplace.

Eventually, you will find you only desire things that are good for your heart and take in things that are uplifting and motivating. Practice this with your entertainment choices and you'll see God honor the decision.

Just to get you started, here are some Christian movies that I've found uplifting and inspiring:

- *Heaven Is For Real*
- *God's Not Dead*
- *Soul Surfer*
- *The Ultimate Gift*
- *Fireproof*
- *Courageous*
- *Son of God*
- *October Baby*
- *The Blind Side*
- *Facing the Giants*
- *When the Game Stands Tall*

FOCUSING ON THE RIGHT ROLE MODELS AND PROTECTING OUR SENSIBILITIES

Negative role models are quickly becoming the new protagonists on television. Many popular shows display bad behavior as normal or even cool. Shows like *Pretty Little Liars* and *Gossip Girl* are just two examples of programs that highlight sin and make it seem desirable. Oftentimes, on many of these dramas, the guy is a jerk and yet he's seen as the one all the girls want. This unhealthy portrayal sets up girls to look for all the wrong qualities in a guy. Do you really want to spend your life with someone who treats you like a second-class citizen? How is that hot? Instead, we should expect that a guy will be kind, caring, and loving if he's boyfriend material.

Once we start to see dangerous guys or immoral behavior as normal and exciting, suddenly a criminal record doesn't seem like that big of a deal. What we chose to entertain ourselves with can only lower our values.

You need to be the one responsible for protecting your heart and mind.

God's world is so much more beautiful than what the media wants you to focus on. If you've seen *Heaven Is For Real* or *God's Not Dead,* just remember how fantastic and light you felt walking out compared to the experience after a horror movie. Isn't it better to leave feeling inspired and desiring more love in the world?

Really check out the ratio of how much time you spend focusing on the positive aspects of God's world and how much you spend in the darker realms of entertainment. Can it be improved? Go on a secular media "fast" and take notes on how you feel. At the end, do you notice you feel more inspired? Godly? Closer to Jesus?

It's really good to check what media you're consuming on a regular basis to keep your heart as pure as possible. If following someone's Instagram, for example, is putting envy in your heart, then it's up to you to unfollow. Check your emotions after your entertainment choices and listen to your soul.

CHAPTER 8

GUARDING YOUR MIND & BODY

Security in Jesus

The Dangers of Sex Before Marriage

GUARDING YOUR MIND & BODY

Whether you're a Christian or not, the temptation and the push to have sex before marriage is everywhere. It's in magazines, on the Internet, and in basically every pop song. In fact, it's so ingrained in our culture that we are almost outsiders if we choose to wait until we're married to have sex. God created us to be set apart from the world, and to be leaders and to stand for what's righteous. Our bodies are just vessels for our souls—and the soul is what lasts forever. If you choose to wait until you're married to have sex, of course it will be difficult (you already know that), but your decision will bring honor to your name and to your future children. It's quite an amazing testimony to be able to say that you waited until you found your Mr. Right. Temptation will be difficult to overcome, but with the right mindset and the refusal to conform, you can do it! And the fight is worth it: If you make one bad decision, that might lead to another, and as the slippery slope continues, you could really hurt your overall self-esteem and come to a point where you don't value yourself at all. Don't settle for a not-so-nice boyfriend over holding out for a godly husband!

The LORD does not look at the things people look at.
People look at the outward appearance,
but the LORD looks at the heart.

1 SAMUEL 16:7

If you want to be pure, you will need to go against worldly culture, and that is difficult. In addition, there's peer pressure to do what's cool or what other people are doing, and it's hard at times to stand for God and do what's honorable.

Your body is a temple for the Holy Spirit, so cherish what God has given you. You want to honor your future husband and your future self. I know it can be difficult to avoid temptation, but I urge you to make good decisions now so in the future you can look back and be happy with your choices.

A singles' pastor used to say, "No one simply falls into bed together before marriage." This is so true. It's a series of smaller choices that lead to bigger mistakes. Things like allowing a make-out session to go too far. Or choosing to be alone in the house together, and especially ignoring the Holy Spirit's promptings.

> *No temptation has overtaken you except what is common to mankind. And God is faithful; he will not let you be tempted beyond what you can bear. But when you are tempted, he will also provide a way out so that you can endure it.*
>
> *1 CORINTHIANS 10:13*

Passion is a very strong and moving emotion. It's easier to walk away when you're at step one than when you are at step three. Don't underestimate temptation's power. Make better, smaller decisions ahead of time.

Once you have had sex, it's easier to have sex again with someone else. You might almost think it doesn't matter now—but it does. God values the life choices you make that bring you closer to Him, and He doesn't want you to go down the wrong path.

I don't want to belittle the fact that these are difficult temptations. It's human nature to want to feel loved, especially as women. You know how the Bible tells women to respect their husbands, but commands men to love their wives? That's because love is what women want to feel from their husbands. When you start looking for "love" and acceptance through sex, you're only pushing away what you really want: To be loved and accepted for who you are on the inside.

Only when you're comfortable with yourself will you attract the right type of guy. If you're not comfortable with yourself, you will be susceptible to changing into someone else to please a guy and eventually relying on him for your happiness. That can be a really dangerous setup because that guy might take the place of God in your life, and no human can love you unconditionally like God can.

If you're feeling really needy and desperate for a boyfriend, I want you to ask yourself what you feel is missing in your life. Figure out what brings you joy. Your future boyfriend or husband wants a girl who has passions and zeal for life outside of him. No one can be your entire world. It's not healthy!

You can always change your habits and your expectations for what you want in a guy. Just because you've dated jerks in the past, it doesn't mean that's all you're capable of attracting. Bad guys may have been part of the learning curve for you, but now you've learned! You will expect more. You are God's princess.

SECURITY IN JESUS

If you're secure in who you are, you'll understand that you deserve to be treated well. If you're still feeling empty or if something seems like it's missing inside, try praying to God and asking Him to fill that void. Act like you're worthy of more until you believe it! You're a daughter of the King! He doesn't give His daughters away like they're tissues. He is a jealous God. A guy has to earn the right to date a daughter of the King. Maybe your father hasn't been protective of you in this way. That doesn't mean that God your Father is the same way.

He knows us intimately and He loves us anyway. Our actions are not hidden from Him, and yet He still loves us with all His heart. We want the marriage relationship to reflect that nature as much as possible. In Ephesians 5:25, God tells us what a husband's responsibilities are, and they are commanded to love their wives as Christ loved the church and gave Himself up for her. Does the guy you're dating have this kind of potential?

Read Psalm 139 until you know it's the truth. It IS the truth. Here's just a portion of this amazing Psalm:

> *If I say, "Surely the darkness will hide me*
> *and the light become night around me,"*
> *even the darkness will not be dark to you;*
> *the night will shine like the day,*
> *for darkness is as light to you.*
> *For you created my inmost being;*
> *you knit me together in my mother's womb.*
> *I praise you because I am fearfully and wonderfully made;*
> *your works are wonderful,*
> *I know that full well.*
>
> *PSALM 139:11–14*

Maybe you think it's too much to ask. I mean, Christ is perfect, right? Of course He is willing to give Himself up for us. I'm going to tell you that there are godly, loving men out there who believe in their roles as protectors. It's awesome to witness in my own husband, and I pray that you choose a future husband who is a man of God, and that he will always cherish and love you. It makes life so much easier if you hold fast to these requirements before you are married.

THE DANGERS OF SEX BEFORE MARRIAGE

I know you've probably heard this all before, but it bears repeating because the repercussions can affect your entire life. Here's a shortlist:

Pregnancy

First, you might get pregnant and not have any financial support or a husband to help care for you and the baby. Being a single mother is infinitely difficult, and more than one guy has promised to be there for an accidental pregnancy only to disappear when it really happened.

I know from experience. My own mother had me when she was only sixteen years old, and my biological father disappeared as soon as I was born. She had to drop out of high school to support us and worked multiple jobs to keep food on the table. I was raised by a single mother my whole life, and I know how tough it can be to not have a child supported by two parents. It's much easier to be a parent to a child when you have a husband who is willing to help you.

Abortion

Being pregnant and alone may also put you at risk to make the choice for abortion. You might think you would never do such a thing, but you'd be surprised how fear can take over in such a situation. Being a parent is a huge responsibility in the best of circumstances, but so much harder when you're on your own and without resources.

If you happen to have already had one, God forgives you—and know that your child is safe in heaven, in Jesus' loving care.

Sexually Transmitted Diseases

Sexually transmitted diseases (STDs) are also cause for concern. Don't think just because someone tells you they're "clean" that they are. It only takes one time to contract a disease, and you'll have to explain to anyone else in your future that you have one. You'll also have to tell your doctors for the rest of your life, and it can be really humiliating, and not what you pictured for yourself at all.

A Change in Your Reputation

A guy might tell his friends that you slept with him, and then your reputation can suffer. He may not be able to keep it to himself. You may think it's not that big of a deal, but if the first guy talked, then the guys you date in the future may expect sex from you. And if you have sex with one guy, it's easier to do it with every single boyfriend afterward. Don't let this happen to you!

As a Christian, sleeping with guys before you're married can harm your faith reputation as well. If you're offering a case for believing in God to others, your behavior can weaken your cause. Make sure your daily choices are pleasing to God so that through those you can be a witness to others.

Biological Consequences

Once you have sex, your body will release oxytocin—the "love and trust" hormone that creates bonding. (It's also the hormone that is released when a mother breastfeeds her child.) This chemical reaction takes place in your body and makes you feel bonded to a guy who may have no feelings for you whatsoever. This can be devastating for a woman.

I don't want you to think if you have made mistakes in your life that you are unredeemable or unworthy. We are human. When faced with temptation, sometimes we don't act as God wants us to. No one is perfect, not even one.

For all have sinned and
fall short of the glory of God.

ROMANS 3:23

Yes, there are consequences to our actions, but in no way does our sin lessen God's love for us.

If we confess our sins, he is faithful and just and will forgive us our sins and purify us from all unrighteousness.

1 JOHN 1:9

If we ask for forgiveness for our sins, His Word claims that we are forgiven. This includes past behaviors we regret.

I also want to add that if you have been raped or sexually abused, you should not feel shame—please know that if that happened to you, it is a tragic result of someone else's sin. Please keep praying to ask God for that burden to be taken from you. He is our comforter and healer. He loves you. In God's eyes, you are still pure because it wasn't your decision and you should not feel shame.

Purity is for our own good. It keeps our soul right with God and helps us stay on the right path and avoid bad decisions. I so encourage you to think deeply about what purity means to you and make good decisions before you're faced with temptation.

BOYS, HEARTBREAK & RELATIONSHIPS

BOYS, HEARTBREAK, AND RELATIONSHIPS

Love is the most enticing, wonderful, thrilling feeling in the world, and maybe that's why heartbreak is so very devastating. After that thrilling joyride of "what could be," sometimes there is the reality of nursing a broken heart.

A broken heart is not something I'd wish on anyone, but there is a chance you may experience one in your life. This is why I feel it's so important to protect your heart as much as possible before marriage. Remember, Scripture tells us above all else to guard our hearts.

Learn to be happy alone. If you're not happy alone, it's impossible to be happy in a relationship. If you think that it's lonely being without a boyfriend, that feeling is only multiplied if you find yourself lonely in a bad marriage and stuck—either because you have children with him or you're against divorce at all costs.

WHAT TO LOOK FOR IN A GUY

One question I often get asked is, "How do I know if he's the one?" So I put together this checklist of what makes a wonderful husband, based on my own personal experience in my marriage:

He is compassionate not only to you, but also to his own parents and strangers he meets. (Just remember, no one is perfect, not even your dream guy.) If he makes a mistake, is he willing to admit it? That's a good sign.

He's drama-free. Soap operas may be fun to watch on television, but they can make for a miserable life if every decision and conversation between you and the boy you're with becomes a drama. Find someone who perhaps enjoys watching drama, but doesn't want to live it!

He's truthful. You can trust his word. He always tells the truth, even in small matters. He's never caught in a lie about a silly thing, because that isn't in his character.

He's hard working. Even if he doesn't have a job, he's someone who is hard working in school and who cares about his grades. Because that type of hard work will carry him through in his first job and beyond. It will be a part of his character

Sluggards do not plow in season;
so at harvest time they look but find nothing.

PROVERBS 20:4

He's patient. If you don't understand something right away, he takes the time to explain it to you, and he does it in a kind way. He doesn't roll his eyes or get annoyed when he has to wait, or speak down to you in frustration.

He's genuine. He knows who he is, and he doesn't change his personality depending on his audience. He has a strong sense of self and a consistent character.

He's loving. Not just physically, but emotionally. He speaks words of love and tells you how much he cares for you and how happy he is to be with you— and means it. Words of affection are very important in a loving relationship.

He pursues you. He doesn't wait for you to take action. By nature, when a man really cares for a woman or wants to be with her, he makes an effort to get to know her. When he does so, he understands that the relationship is something he truly wants and he's committed. A man should make the first move. I know that's controversial, but it's how I feel.

Most important of all, he's a man of God. He's accountable to God, and puts his hope and faith in the Lord Jesus Christ.

Even if you were in a bad relationship, you must forgive yourself and move on. I'm grateful that I learned from my bad relationships. Afterward, I prayed and made a commitment to never settle for a man who didn't love God and cherish me. After recognizing that I would never tolerate bad behavior in a boyfriend again, I focused on becoming the best me possible and was content with being single and in a healthy place when my amazing husband, Eric, came along.

I LIKE A GUY, BUT HE DOESN'T RETURN THE FEELING. SHOULD I MOVE ON?

If a guy you're interested in isn't returning your attentions, and he's made it clear, it's a sign that he's not the one for you. You need to move on and not waste your precious time. Instead of focusing on a one-sided relationship, you could use the time you're single to grow closer to God, trust His plan, and stay on the path toward meeting the right guy for you. What if you were dating a guy who wasn't your future husband, and Mr. Right came along and you weren't available?

SHOULD I EVER ASK HIM OUT?

I'm old school here. I believe that if a guy can't pursue you, how will the relationship work? You want someone who is willing to risk having his feelings out there and to take a chance in order to be with you, because that shows commitment and that he sees a future with you. It's also biblical. In the Bible, it's always the man who pursues the wife, and in many cases he pursues her relentlessly.

In the book of Ruth, for instance, Boaz shows all the characteristics of a strong, protective husband when he pursues Ruth. When he first sees her, his interest is piqued. He is the overseer of all the harvesters, and Ruth has been left alone with her mother-in-law to fend for herself. She asks Boaz if she can just glean the leftovers from the wheat so that she and her mother-in-law can eat.

Boaz, being a real man of God, immediately wants to protect and care for her, and he has a desire to care for her. He doesn't want her grabbing the leftovers. He wants everything for her, and the right man will want that for you.

As in the Bible, if a relationship is meant to be, God will make it happen. There is no sense in forcing something that isn't meant for you. You want a man who treats you with the kindness and loving protection of Boaz—who soon drops all the pretenses of Ruth working for him, and then goes out of his way later to make sure she can be his wife (see Ruth 4:1–12), and marries her.

Girls, just like the story of Ruth, God wants your full dedication and reliance on Him. I believe once God has our full attention, He will bless us in great ways; and if you're praying to meet your future husband, you'll be ready for a godly relationship.

HOW DO I KNOW IF HE'S THE ONE?

- He's the nicest guy you've ever met.

- When you're with him, you feel totally comfortable being your true self.

- He puts you first in the relationship. (Again, this is the biblical model!)

- He treats you like a gentleman should.

- He's respectful.

- He listens to your needs and wants to make you happy.

- He loves God like you do.

- You can't wait to be with him again.

- He has nothing but good things to say about you to his friends and family and doesn't tolerate someone speaking ill of you.

- You feel confirmation from the Holy Spirit. If you hear or feel any reservations, God has something better for you.

- You're clear-headed about your choices. You're not blinded by sheer emotion.

Husbands, love your wives,
just as Christ loved the church
and gave himself up for her.

EPHESIANS 5:25

WHAT TO AVOID IN A GUY (THE WARNING SIGNS!)

When we're young, it can be really easy to tell ourselves someone is "perfect" or our "soul mate" because he's cute. Obviously, there's more to finding the right man.

Don't feel like just because you're not ready to get married that these warning signs below are null and void. Who we pick as young women can really determine what we settle for later in life, so make sure your standards are high right from the start. Here are some red flag behaviors:

He's inconsistent. The right kind of guy has a consistent personality. He's not one way when he's with his friends and another way when he's with you. If he's nice to you when you're alone, but a jerk when his friends are around, he's too concerned with what other people think. He's not confidant in who he is, and you want someone who has your back. This isn't the godly man God has in mind for you.

He's rude to people. If a guy is rude to others, it won't be long until he's rude to you too. Also, don't tolerate bad behavior, because it can harm your own reputation if he's rude to others. If you're with him, that will reflect on you.

He lies about little things. If he lies about things that don't matter, you'll never be able to trust him about things that do. It becomes a part of his character.

He never takes responsibility for his actions. He never apologizes or says he's sorry. When we're wrong, it's an important part of our character that we say we're sorry and try to make amends for behavior. Someone who is not able to say he's sorry blames other people for the trouble he finds himself in. Imagine trying to work out an issue with someone who is never wrong! This is one of the leading causes of fights among couples, because arguments never get settled when one person can't say they're sorry. Disagreements and even decisions can't be made with a person who is unwilling to take responsibility for their choices.

He pressures you to do things you don't want to do. We've all been given a conscience. When our conscience is pinging, and someone else doesn't respect that, we can be led down a wrong path and compromise our values. A good boyfriend recognizes that you are separate from him and respects your morals and what you do or don't want to do.

He doesn't acknowledge what you say. A true relationship is two-sided and allows for you to speak and have an opinion. If it's never your turn to speak, or worse yet, you do speak and are ignored, this is a major red flag. This is probably a guy who doesn't respect women.

He is selfish. He always wants to do what he wants to do regarding plans and doesn't take into account what you would like to do. It's great to go out and watch him tear up the mud in motocross, but once in a while, maybe you want to see the latest *Hunger Games* movie. Later on, when you're a mom, selfish men are just like having another child.

When you want to buy something nice for yourself, he mocks it or judges you for your choices. Does he question little things like how you spend your money or what you choose to watch on TV? There is no relaxing with someone who is constantly judging you over little things. You need the freedom to just be you or you'll be in "fight or flight" mode all the time, and that is exhausting! The longer you tolerate bad behavior, the more you accept and the more it becomes normal to you. Don't let it get started!

He is someone who tries to isolate you from friends and family. If a guy is territorial and feels anxious when you spend time with friends and family, he probably has some deeper issues. You can never fill someone else's needs if they're counting on you to make them feel good about themselves. This kind of guy can easily turn into a controlling boyfriend.

He gives you subtle put-downs. If a guy offers subtle put-downs that make you feel bad about yourself, this is a way of gaining control over your self-confidence. Be very careful with this kind of thing because this person can use information that you give them in confidence to gain an advantage over you. Also, he may try to make you feel unworthy of someone else by constantly criticizing you or putting you down.

He's shady. Direct questions deserve answers. If you find that a guy avoids direct answers or returns your questions with ones of his own, he's probably incapable of being fully honest. As long as you're not asking something too personal, you deserve an answer. Also, be wary of the kind of guy who accuses you of being paranoid when you ask him a simple question. Keep in mind, some guys are more thoughtful than others and he may take longer to answer a question. That doesn't mean he's shady or lying. It may simply mean he's more analytical and that he's thinking about his answer.

He's not fun to be around. If you find that your relationship is always focused around "heavy" issues and you're not having a good time, it may be time to move on.

You're not yourself around him. You start to realize you turn into someone else when you're with him. This might be you trying to be someone's perfect girlfriend, and it's a sign he isn't for you. Don't change who you are in order to get him to like you more. Because who you are (your personality and values) will be what makes you someone's perfect girlfriend and perhaps future wife. I can testify that God has so much better for you if you let go and stop struggling to be perfect. This might be something as little as acting like you're into a band that you're not really into. Or dressing in a certain way that is more his style than yours. Even feeling like you have to have makeup on or look perfect to be around him. You are already perfect in God's eyes.

He is a lazy guy who isn't motivated to better himself. The truth is, women need to feel a sense of safety and security when we have children, and that's why it's important to have a guy who recognizes providing. You may be too young to worry about this now, but it's a good pattern to get into looking for a guy who is motivated to build a solid life for himself and who he marries.

DEAL BREAKERS

The following are characteristics that you should never tolerate in any boyfriend. These are deal breakers that need to be addressed in one way, and one way only: *By breaking it off!*

He's a cheater. The old adage is true. Once a cheater, always a cheater. Never tolerate this behavior. It's also not okay if he has a wandering eye and makes you feel like he's not fully present. You're better than that, and you will be more than enough for the right guy.

He's physically or verbally abusive. This is not ever love. These guys don't change for anyone. You cannot love any guy enough to fix these issues. He has underlying anger/rage issues that have nothing to do with you. Move on quickly. Learn how to be alone if necessary, but never put up with someone like this. Your future husband should be kind and respectful, because your children will not learn to respect authority if their father models disrespect. It's one of the worst traits you can pass onto your children, so think ahead.

If you are in an abusive relationship, enlist the help of a trusted adult or church leader, or call an abuse hotline. You can find confidential help here: 1.800.799.SAFE (7233) or 1.800.787.3224 (TTY).

HEARTBREAK

When I was twenty, I was in a relationship with an atheist and thought it was no big deal. Even though I hadn't yet given my life over to Jesus at this point in my life, I never was an "unbeliever," and I still believed that God was real. So there were times I would talk about God with this boyfriend. When I told him that God in fact made the universe, stars, the earth and everything around us, he would make fun of me and tell me I was stupid. Thankfully we broke up after a year and a half of dating (way too long) but at least God closed that door. This guy actually told me one of the reasons he didn't want to be with me anymore was because he thought I wasn't as intelligent as he was. Can you imagine if I ended up staying with him, what a completely different path my life would be on right now? Who knows, any semblance of faith I might have had probably would have disappeared, and I wouldn't be writing this book let alone reaching thousands of teen girls telling them about Jesus. You see, God tells us explicitly in the Bible that we are not to be paired with people who are unbelievers. Because not only can it hinder your own relationship with God, but you could also be losing the opportunity to save someone else through your own faith and testimony. God doesn't want us spending time with people who could in the end damage our relationship with Him!

> *Do not be yoked together with unbelievers. For what do righteousness and wickedness have in common? Or what fellowship can light have with darkness?*
>
> *2 CORINTHIANS 6:14*

If I had only listened to the promptings of the Holy Spirit when I was in that relationship, it would have saved me a lot of time and unnecessary heartbreak. If you're currently getting promptings in your heart regarding the relationship you're in, do not ignore them! God is trying to reach you and give you a message. For instance, if you're afraid to be alone, you might be falling victim to fear, and we should never make decisions on who we date based on fears for the future.

It's also important to keep your own dreams alive and not let a relationship define them for you. When you're with the right guy, he will want to help you achieve your dreams. The marriage relationship is described as two becoming one, so you don't want someone who competes with you. You're on the same team!

Trust me; you never need someone who makes you feel less than you are. Friends and boyfriends should give you the benefit of the doubt and think highly of you— not try to tell you who you are. If someone says you need to change yourself in order to stay in the relationship, and it doesn't align with what you know to be true, then don't believe this twisted version of who you are.

I've forgiven this ex-boyfriend and myself. I think it's really important to forgive those who have hurt you in the past, so that you don't harbor resentment and anger. It's very unhealthy to carry around resentment. Clearly, I didn't forget this bad behavior. I didn't forget that I never wanted to be called stupid again, and I've since realized he had his own issues, but that didn't make it okay for him to say the things he did to me. Forgiving is healthy, but I learned to never allow that to happen to me again.

The right man will love you for exactly who you are. Your quirks and mistakes won't be deal breakers. One of my favorite love stories in the Bible is that of Jacob and his unwavering love for Rachel. When he first sees her as a shepherdess with her flock, Jacob is smitten from the start. He rolls the heavy stone from the well and waters her flock for her and goes straight to her father for her hand in marriage.

> *Rachel had a lovely figure and was beautiful. Jacob was in love with Rachel and said, "I will work for you seven years in return for your younger daughter Rachel."*
>
> *GENESIS 29:17–18*

But Jacob's new father-in-law had to marry off his older daughter first, so he tricked Jacob into marrying the wrong sister. Devastated by Laban's betrayal, Jacob—being a man of character—stayed married to Leah, but agreed to work another seven years for Rachel. That story is just so romantic in that Jacob knew immediately that Rachel was for him, and nothing stopped him from pursuing and marrying the woman he loved. I want that for you! (Without the second wife, obviously. Times have changed!)

There are many brilliant women who have fallen into the trap of unhealthy relationships, so don't judge yourself if you're there. Just get out if you're being harmed physically or emotionally.

How Do I Deal with My Broken Heart?

If your heart has been broken, now is the time you really need to lean on Him. First, God is with you during this incredibly tough time. He can heal broken hearts. He makes all things new. But it does take time. When you put your hopes and dreams into a future with someone, the loss of that person can represent a loss of your dreams.

> *He heals the brokenhearted*
> *and binds up their wounds.*
>
> PSALM 147:3

If a guy broke your heart, he wasn't the one for you. I know that doesn't lessen your pain or make you feel better immediately, but it is the truth. When the right guy comes along, he will cherish your heart and want to protect and care for it.

Cry it out. There's nothing wrong with crying and letting out your frustration. Don't rebound with another guy or jump into another relationship right away. You need time to heal. It's okay to feel the pain. Wish the guy well and find peace in your heart. Grief is a process. Allow yourself ample time for it.

Don't call him! Sometimes, when we're hurt, we want to call the person who hurt us. I mean, you were so close, right? You just want him to help soothe your broken heart. But he's not the one to do it. A clean break is healthier—harder, but healthier. Find other activities to fill your time or call a friend if you're tempted to call him.

Don't live in the past. Grief is hard when you're dealing with the dreams you thought you might have had with your ex-boyfriend. Allow yourself to walk through the pain and don't look backward as if the breakup was a mistake. Look forward to your dreams for yourself. If you're continually thinking he might come back, you'll stop yourself from moving ahead.

Assess what was wrong and what was right. When you've had some space, ask yourself what you really liked about that relationship and what made it less than perfect. Being realistic will help you in your next relationship.

HOW DO I AVOID BAD RELATIONSHIPS?

If you've had a bad relationship, don't beat yourself up over it. It may have been a learning path for you. The important thing is not to let it happen again, or at all if you've been spared this type of pain so far. Here are some tips for keeping yourself from bad relationships:

Listen to the people who love you. Friends and family have the power of perspective. They're not emotionally involved with your boyfriend, so they have a better view of how it may be affecting you negatively. They see the flaws that you cannot if you're blinded by emotions.

Don't settle for less because your parents did. If your parents don't have the best relationship, don't repeat the pattern or believe that you need to settle. Make a list of what you don't like about the adult relationships you've seen. What parts did you want to emulate? Sometimes, a little analytical thinking can save us from learning the hard way later.

Understand that you're worthy of a healthy relationship. On *ProjectInspired.com*, we say to date with intention and not desperation. The best way to go about this is to like who you are. Learn to love who you are when you're alone and single. Embrace your individual characteristics that make you, you!

HOW CAN I TELL IF HIS FAITH IS REAL?

A boy who has a genuine faith will have a heart to do what is right before God. That doesn't mean he will be perfect, but it does mean that when he makes a mistake, he is able to own up to it and take responsibility.

You will see his acts of goodness. His faith will be more than something uttered from his mouth. It will show in his actions. "In the same way, faith by itself, if it not accompanied by action, is dead" (James 2:17).

Pay attention: Watch how he treats his mom, his sisters—even waitresses and complete strangers. Is he respectful? The way he treats others is eventually the way he'll treat you!

He's someone you like as-is. Don't expect to change a guy. He is who he is, and while he may be capable of pretending for a time, eventually, the real him will come out, so make sure you're falling in love with the real person, not an imaginary hero you've created in your mind.

He's joyful! You can't make another person happy if they are not happy in themselves. Everyone is prone to dark times in life; you just need to make sure this isn't the core of his personality. He needs to possess a certain amount of joy that comes only from God!

CHAPTER 10

DATING TIPS FOR PROJECT INSPIRED GIRLS

When Is It Okay to Date?

Dating Tips

All of My Friends Are Dating, but I'm Not. Now what?

WHEN IS IT OKAY TO DATE?

God instituted marriage for companionship, but He also wanted couples to come together with the idea of raising godly families. Many people believe (and please honor your parents if this is their belief system!) that you should only date when you're marriage-minded.

I tend to be more on the conservative side of this issue. Dating for fun isn't what God had in mind when He introduced Adam to Eve. He set them together with a purpose: to populate the earth.

While there is no specific age to begin dating, I recommend waiting awhile. Although it may seem tough, especially if all your friends are dating, it will keep you from dealing with unnecessary temptation and heartbreak. Personally, I'd say eighteen, because at this age you're legally an adult and you're either done with, or almost done with, high school.

NICOLE'S TIP

I'm a big believer in group dates, especially the first couple of times you go out with a person. You won't feel tempted to kiss him, and it's just more comfortable when it's not one-on-one early in the relationship.

. . .

DATING TIPS

#1: Try to date guys with similar interests.

Of course, your hobbies may not be exactly the same, but your values and lifestyle should be similar. You probably don't want an extreme bungee jumper, for example, if you're a quiet, reading type of person. Also, if he's a vegetarian and steak is your favorite thing to eat, this might set you up for conflict. You'll also want to make sure you're on the same page about things. If you're an animal lover and he's not, that might create arguments later on when you want to get a pet. If you envision children in your future, you need to make sure he does too. If he only sees himself having a hamster to take care of, he's most likely not the right guy for you. Unless you're really into hamsters too.

#2: Be you!

Don't compromise who you are in order to be accepted by the one you're trying to win over! God made you completely unique, with your own special qualities, your distinctive traits, and your natural beauty. Don't trade in your values and your character for your date. You are worthy! Your future boyfriend or husband will accept you as you are. If he doesn't and tries to change you, that's a warning sign that you shouldn't be in that relationship.

#3: Don't settle for anything less than God's best!

Recognize what you want in a boyfriend. What type of character does he have? Is he easy going, intelligent, and adventurous? Does he have strong family values? Don't waste your time with anyone who doesn't treat you with utmost respect. *You deserve the best because you are God's princess!*

#4: Stay passionate about your life!

If you keep your primary focus on God and stay active in the things you love to do, your date will see that and be much more intrigued by you. So don't give up your dreams and your goals just because you're dating someone new. Your passions and interests can bring something fresh to the relationship and you can inspire him as well!

#5: Compliment each other!

Many times, people are quick to point out what their boyfriend did wrong, how they wish that person would change, etc. If your partner is doing something good and you like it, make sure they know! Tell them or write them a nice note. Your thoughts can't benefit your loved one if you don't express it to them.

My husband and I often leave little notes for each other on the sink in the morning. It helps make the day more special and it's a reminder of how much we love each other.

#6: Avoid temptation.

Don't put yourself in a situation where temptation is harder to deal with. Stay in a public location, preferably with another person along. If you know hanging out with him in your parents' basement will lead to temptation, go out and do an activity together that you both love or explore your city, like I mentioned in the friendship chapter. He might not want to have a manicure day with you, but I'm sure he'd love to try some fun activities!

#7: Let your date meet your parents.

They're more likely to approve of your boyfriend if they know him. If they don't approve, listen to their warning. Most likely, they have their reasons—even if you can't understand those reasons from your perspective. Plus, if a guy really cares about you, he'll want to meet your parents and want for them to like him.

#8: Avoid committing too soon.

Don't force a guy to commit to a relationship after one date. Take it slow, get to know each other, and let the relationship grow at its own pace.

#9: Be sure your boyfriend is interested in marriage.

If a guy sees himself being a player for the rest of his life, he has no business being with a beautiful Christian girl like you. He should see marriage in his future. However, you don't want to scare him off by picking out rings and showing him your favorite wedding gowns in magazines. Don't rush into anything, as it can scare guys off, and dating is meant to be a time for you to determine if you want a life with this person. Enjoy the time of being friends and getting to know one another.

#10: Don't stop hanging out with your friends!

You don't want to neglect your friendships just because of one guy. Trust me that it's important to have girl time, even if you are super close with your boyfriend! Plus, your boyfriend will have a chance to be with his friends as well. And it's always good to have more people to rely on—if you do break up with your boyfriend, you'll have your friends still there so that you can turn to them to help heal your broken heart.

ALL OF MY FRIENDS ARE DATING, BUT I'M NOT. NOW WHAT?

Take the time to remember who you are. Your self-worth shouldn't be determined by who you're dating or if you're dating. You're God's girl and He's pleased you're choosing to put off dating until the time is right.

Spend more time with God. God has given us the Holy Spirit to help us get through difficult times in our lives. When you're feeling especially lonely, that would be a good time to communicate with God. Pull out your Bible and read some passages that remind you about how special you are to God and how much He loves you. I love the daily devotional Jesus Calling because it keeps me on track and focused on God's Word every day.

Meet new people. Of course you don't want to stop being friends with your old friends just because they're dating and you're not, but you do want to find some peers to hang out with who have similar interests. If your current friends are spending most of their time with their new boyfriends, then you should focus on finding new and different things to do too. Find some girls (and guys) who are into some of the same things you are and have fun with these new people. Who knows—you might find your Prince Charming in the process (if you're interested in dating).

Set new goals. Choose some things that you like to do and practice them to become better. Or perhaps you've always wanted to learn the French language; take the time to learn it and become bilingual, or trilingual if you already know two languages! (That would be amazing!) Maybe you love to design clothes. Take a sewing class and start small with pillowcases or tops! Or you could possibly start your own blog and master the art of writing and creating content online. In the process of pursuing your goals, you'll discover more about yourself, your passions, and what you're good at!

Dating is a huge topic, and I want you to remember that no one else is needed to complete you, because you are whole in Jesus! And if you do want a relationship, remember to keep praying and give it up to God, as He knows the right timing for your life and He wants you to trust and rely on Him to bring a godly man into your life. You can live your life fully and abundantly with the love from your friends, family, and chosen passions. And remember that when you pursue your goals or a new project, that could be the activity where you meet your future husband! So take advantage of opportunities and get out there and explore, because you won't get into a relationship from staying inside all day! You are blessed, loved, and a worthy girl of God. Your future boyfriend or husband will be lucky to be with you!

I hope you remember that no one else is needed to complete you. And while you're waiting for God to bring you Mr. Right, never miss an opportunity to live your life fully and abundantly. I know it can be painful to be alone, but God is with you, even in the dark times.

CHAPTER 11

OVERCOMING DEPRESSION

My Friend Is Cutting Herself.
How Can I Help Her?

Footprints in the Sand

OVERCOMING DEPRESSION

Depression is a very real, often chemical or hormonal reaction that can skew our belief system so that we feel unworthy and unloved, even if there is no logical reason to feel such a way.

It's a heartbreaking myth that Christians are immune to depression, and one that can really harm our emotional well-being and prevent us from getting help for the problem. There can be a lot of shame with depression. The idea is that if we were really Christians, we wouldn't have those feelings, right?

I can testify from my own experience that this is completely untrue. I can also state that if I hadn't gone through the deep, dark depression that I experienced, I might still be on the wrong road and living a life without meaning.

Because God used my broken state of being, He was able to mold me into someone who needed Him and who finally understood His plan for my life. Without that dark time, I might have remained on the same path and not let God take control of my life. But while I'm grateful for what my trials brought in the end, I wouldn't wish depression on anyone. It can be a terrible, overwhelming place, and the worst of it is that it feels so real.

Maybe you or a friend has suffered from depression after you became a Christian. That doesn't make it any less devastating. Nor does it make you "not a real Christian." Remember, Satan is a liar and often takes advantage of a depressed state to tell us lies so that it's impossible to believe the truth.

If you have a friend who suffers from depression, never tell them that they "shouldn't feel that way" or to "get over it." I promise you, they don't want to feel the way they do, but wanting to feel happy and normal again doesn't stop the intrusive thoughts from coming to them. Be there for them and encourage them to get the help they need.

God never wants to see us suffer, but he can use our challenges, including depression, to make us even stronger Christians, like in my case. Girls, I know this is true because I lived it. Many times, He uses our pain to ultimately lead us to Him. When things seem impossible and extremely hard, that's when we need Him the most. Trusting His truths, even when we can't see outside the overwhelming darkness, will make us stronger. I know how easy it is to give into the lies during those times, but look at God's Truth in the Bible:

Blessed are the poor in spirit, for theirs is the kingdom of heaven.
Blessed are those who mourn, for they will be comforted.
Blessed are the meek, for they will inherit the earth.
Blessed are those who hunger and thirst for righteousness,
for they will be filled.
Blessed are the merciful, for they will be shown mercy.
Blessed are the pure in heart, for they will see God.
Blessed are the peacemakers, for they will be called children of God.
Blessed are those who are persecuted because of righteousness,
for theirs is the kingdom of heaven.
Blessed are you when people insult you, persecute you
and falsely say all kinds of evil against you because of me.
Rejoice and be glad, because great is your reward in heaven,
for in the same way they persecuted the prophets who were before you.

MATTHEW 5:3–12

Read Psalms during your down days. King David, who wrote many of the psalms, went through dark times and he came out triumphantly. David was sad, angry, and expressed a full range of emotion! God is not afraid of our emotions. He won't back away from us because He can't handle our innermost thoughts. Sometimes, our emotions may be too much for others to deal with, but God is not like others.

If you're depressed, please don't isolate yourself. Isolation makes the lies speak louder.

I know that I couldn't see how it could be better at the time, so my advice to you is: Don't trust those feelings. God is holding you in the palm of His hand and He will heal you and get you through this challenging time. If you're going through this, you have to keep moving forward in faith because your feelings may betray you. I know that, looking back, God was with me, but I didn't feel it at the time. I felt alone and hopeless. I can't stress enough that this feeling is temporary. It takes a lot of prayer and perhaps the help of a doctor or a therapist's intervention, but I promise you, it will get better.

I can remember how it felt, and I now reflect back and use that pain to speak to others. We need more than ever to run to God in the midst of depression, rather than turn away from our faith. We have to trust the promises of the Bible. Like this one:

"For I know the plans I have for you," declares the LORD,
"plans to prosper you and not to harm you,
plans to give you hope and a future."

JEREMIAH 29:11

Looking back, I now realize that God used my challenges to make me a stronger individual. In nature, the substance of coal, when exposed to extreme pressure, creates a beautiful diamond! You might be under extreme pressure now, but God can use that to make you into the sparkling, unique person that He wants you to become.

I can't emphasize enough that when your faith is renewed, you know you can overcome anything. Some of the greatest achievements on record were made by people who had to suffer really tough circumstances to become who they were meant to be.

Winston Churchill, prime minster of Britain during World War II, was said to suffer from what he called "the black dog." Born into a family with a genetic predisposition for mental illness, his struggle and depression allowed him to see threats that others, without that awareness of darkness, couldn't see. Specifically, he foresaw that Adolph Hitler posed a danger to society and harbored sinister intentions. Other leaders of the time thought that Hitler could be trusted to do what was right, while Churchill saw the real truth. It has been said that if Churchill did not suffer from depression, we might all be speaking German today. If we allow Him to use us, God will use even our darkest days for His glory.

Don't underestimate your own struggles and how God might use them for good in the future. He has a plan for all of us—and if we listen and trust His plan for our lives, then His vision will far exceed our own dreams for the future. When we are in the valley of our struggles, it's pretty impossible to see the plans God has for us. In truth, all we want is to make the pain stop. But I know that for myself, I can look back and see the good that my own depression and struggles brought me.

In the book of 1 Samuel, a woman named Hannah, is married to Elkanah, who had another wife. The other wife had a child, but Hannah couldn't have any and she was so depressed and cried out to God.

Her husband didn't understand. He loved his wife Hannah, and her sadness grieved him. So he said to her, "Hannah, why are you weeping? Why don't you eat? Why are you downhearted? Don't I mean more to you than ten sons?" (1 Samuel 1:8).

Because the Lord had closed Hannah's womb,
her rival kept provoking her to irritate her.
This went on year after year. Whenever Hannah
went up to the house of the LORD, her rival
provoked her till she wept and would not eat.

1 SAMUEL 1:6–7

Sometimes, men just don't get it. Nowhere is this truer than with Hannah's husband.

To be bullied by her husband's other wife must have been excruciating for Hannah. The one thing Hannah wanted was denied, while her rival was blessed with many children and taunted her with the fact. People can be so mean!

What's incredible is that in her deep anguish, and weeping bitterly, Hannah prayed to the Lord. She vowed that if God gave her a son, she would offer him to the Lord for all the days of his life. I love that Hannah didn't return bitterness for bitterness. She still had faith and still prayed! She went so far as to offer up this son knowing that if God honored her request, her son would be for a higher purpose. Haven't we all tried to make deals with God in our prayers? Sometimes, they work.

Perhaps Hannah's story has served other parents who waited and prayed for a while just like she did. Hannah wasn't just waiting and praying. God was preparing her heart so she would be the mother He needed to raise the prophet Samuel. God prepares our hearts when we are praying for our heart's desires. Remember that, He has a purpose even in our unanswered prayers.

Hannah's son, Samuel, was a prophet and one of the last judges. He was meant to be a strong leader for God. Sometimes, we have to keep praying despite our own hopelessness.

We cannot let our feelings separate us from God. In my own life, God blessed me with our child, Elijah, after I gave my life to the Lord, and I believe He needed me prepared to be a Christian mother so I could raise a godly son who loves Jesus like I do. Remember, God's timing in your life is not only for your own good, but for your future children's, if you have any.

Here are some tips that will help you during a tough time in your life:

First, tell someone. Don't isolate yourself. Get the help you need—maybe that's telling a parent or a trusted adult, such as a pastor. Maybe it's taking the step to call a doctor for help. The important thing is not to ignore it! Depression can be a chemical imbalance, and if it's severe, you should definitely ask your parents to seek medical help.

> *The thief comes only to steal and kill and destroy;*
> *I have come that they may have life, and have it to the full.*
>
> *JOHN 10:10*

Take Small Steps! Remember, the best thing you can do when you're depressed is take it day by day. Don't worry about what next week will hold or what the future will look like. Just worry about getting through one day at a time. Examples of small steps:

- Call a friend that day.
- Go outside and feel the sunshine.
- Force yourself to take a warm shower and use a yummy-smelling body wash.
- Get dressed in something nice even if you're just going across the street.
- Apply makeup even if it feels pointless.
- Read the Bible. God's Word is living, and His truth will comfort you during your darkest days.
- Exercise! Even if it's for ten minutes. Remember, it's all about small steps.

Force yourself to do something that feels hard. You'll feel joy at accomplishing something and, hopefully, that will push you to try another step. Don't be discouraged. Do the work to find out where your depression is coming from. Is it chemical? Emotional? Situational? Look for its source and work with medical professionals if necessary.

Depression is not of God; so don't succumb to the lies. Remember, Jesus came to bring you a joyful and abundant life of fulfillment. He doesn't want you living in this kind of pain. He has an important plan for you and He wants you healed from this, so don't give into it.

Confide in close friends to pray for you. Ask your church's prayer chain, if you don't feel you have friends you can tell. You don't have to tell them specifics, just that you are going through something challenging and need extra prayer. Sometimes just saying to someone else, "I'm struggling" will lift some of the burden from your shoulders.

Three of my favorite books, which I really encourage you to read if you're feeling depressed and in need of hope, are:

Godforsaken: Bad Things Happen. Is There a God Who Cares? Here's Proof by Dinesh D'Souza. It helped answer some really tough questions for me and I found it so useful.

Walking with God through Pain and Suffering by Timothy Keller is another must-read if you're dealing with suffering and sadness. Keller is an amazing author. I also loved his book *The Reason for God: Belief in the Age of Skepticism.*

MY FRIEND IS CUTTING HERSELF. HOW CAN I HELP HER?

Cutting is a very complicated issue and most likely not something we can handle alone. It's a compulsive issue that requires your friend to get professional intervention to help her get through the emotions that are causing her to harm herself.

It can be really difficult and confusing to watch a friend hurt herself. You need to be supportive, but you also absolutely cannot hide "her secret." You need to confide in a trusted adult who can get her the help she needs. This might feel like a betrayal of your friend's trust, but wouldn't you rather have an angry friend than one who isn't there? Sometimes, doing what's right is really, really hard.

Cutting or self-harm is damaging behavior that can be very addictive. People who struggle with this must learn how to deal with difficult emotions in a new way. That isn't easy! Once we learn a "coping" method, we often return to it without even thinking. Remember, though, cutting and self-harm aren't coping. They're only avoiding the more difficult issues that need to be addressed.

During the process of learning to trade cutting for something else, your friend needs to be held accountable to someone else—preferably a professional. Remember, this is like any addiction where a person turns to the compulsion or damaging activity rather than feel hard emotions or handle traumatic situations. Your friend may not be at a place where she can stop on her own, so please don't judge her, but do look for ways to get her help. Often, people who are harming themselves are subconsciously letting others know that they need help, even if they can't verbalize it.

What you can do is be there for her and support her as she seeks alternative ways to soothe herself. Making a list of soothing activities might help, such as taking a warm bubble bath or reading a Christian book—actions that help her avoid the compulsion to cut and instead do something else. Having a list ready can be beneficial when she's in the throes of painful emotions.

Cutting and the underlying causes are not easy to fix. Again, please don't give up on your friend or keep your friend's suffering to yourself. If you have any concerns about a friend self-harming or you are considering harming yourself, reach out immediately!! Call the Suicide Prevention hotline at 1-800-273-TALK.

I don't mean to sound heartless here, but the Bible does present suicide as a sin, so it is never the godly way out of pain, and it is so permanent. Suicide is never presented as virtuous in the Bible. (Judas Iscariot is just one example!)

The reason I believe it's a sin is because the Bible tells us in the Ten Commandments that we are not to murder. God values life—yours as well as someone else's. So please don't commit this desperate act and cause never-ending pain to those around you. You have your entire life in front of you, and while things might seem impossible, nothing is worth giving away the life God has graced you with.

It is so painful for me to see so many beautiful, gorgeous young faces on my website and to know a few out there are thinking these thoughts at times. God wants so much for you. Remember, over and over in the Bible, it tells you He has you in the palm of His hand and that He is with you every step of the way.

The LORD is close to the brokenhearted,
and saves those who are crushed in spirit.

PSALM 34:18

Depression is very real. It doesn't make you a failure. It doesn't make you less of a Christian. It means you're in need of help. Often, as Christians, we want to be the one doing for other people, so when we need something for ourselves, it can be very hard to ask for help. If you're feeling down, read this beautiful poem. I love it.